the
parker lifetime treasury
of
mystic
and occult powers

the
parker lifetime treasury
of
mystic
and Occult powers

**Compiled and Edited
by
Theodor Laurence**

Parker Publishing Company   West Nyack, N.Y.

© 1978 by

Parker Publishing Company, Inc.

West Nyack, New York

All rights reserved. No part of this book
may be reproduced in any form or by any
means, without permission in writing
from the publisher.

10   9   8   7

This book is a reference work based on research by the author. The
opinions expressed herein are not necessarily those of or endorsed by
the Publisher.

Library of Congress Cataloging in Publication Data
Main entry under title:

The Parker lifetime treasury of mystic and occult powers.

1. Occult sciences. 2. Success. I. Laurence,
Theodor. II. Parker Publishing Company, West Nyack,
N. Y. III. Title: Mystic and occult powers.
BF1411.P37   133   78-17300

Printed in the United States of America

PREVIOUS BOOKS BY LAURENCE:

To the businessman with a heart:

Earl Mitchell

WHAT THIS BOOK WILL DO FOR YOU

POWER — that's what this book is about.
PERSONAL POWER — that's what this book offers you.
SHAPE-SHIFTING, FATE-TRANSFORMING, LIFE-ENRICHING, PERSONAL POWER — that's what you will gain page after page!

THE BIRTH OF YOUR POWER BOOK

In recent years the accent has been on groups, organizations, masses, and collective bodies. The individual as a self-contained, self-regulating, self-determining unit of personal power has been undermined, suppressed, and ignored. It is time to right this wrong. It is time you as a person had the opportunity to avail yourself of potent and effective personal power—power to change circumstances, renovate conditions, and revolutionize your own life.

There *are* keys to this miraculous power. They are all here, right now, in your hands. Until now, these dynamic keys, embodying the secrets of mystic and occult Masters, have been for the most part published separately. For the first time anywhere, and for the benefit of unintimidated individuals, these secret techniques for success and happiness are brought together in one single, miracle-working volume.

The Parker Publishing Company determined to glean the best and most successful occult and mystic powers from numerous sources and combine them into one great treasury, one vast mine of knowledge, one master plan for personal success, one universal guide-map to a fuller, richer life. That accumulation of power is now in your hands, in this book. It has been my pleasure to undertake the task of presenting between these two covers a success program designed to bring you—quickly and easily—the very power you need in this day and age of anti-individualism. Careful organization and editing (always with *you* in mind) have produced this book of personal power, the first and only system that incorporates gems of mystic and occult techniques (in *easy, modern language*) into a powerful, practical program for achieving health, wealth, success, and happiness.

A TREASURY OF POWERS IS YOURS

In this book you will learn to use 13 new and magical powers—13 remarkable treasures of occult and mystic know-how for getting what you want out of life—quickly and easily. I settled on the number 13 deliberately—the occult number virtually *vibrates* with power! Once you begin to use the 13 powers provided for you, a veritable treasure-trove of riches, joy, and pleasure will be yours. And you will be on your way toward a new life of happiness, fulfillment, accomplishment, satisfaction, and gratification—a new life of POWER!

YOUR 13 POSITIVE OCCULT AND MYSTIC POWERS

What are the 13 Powers of which I speak?

It has been my experience that when a person sincerely desires to be an individual—to think for himself, to march to his own drummer, and to achieve success unheard of by others—certain abilities and qualities must be his. Every successful individual I know possesses and enjoys:

Mental Power
Psychic Power
The Power of Luck
Miracle Power
Healing Power
The Power of Command
Magic Power
Occult Power
Astral Power
The Power of Love
Money Power
Achievement Power
The Power of Self-Protection

Count them. There are 13! And these 13 wonder-working Powers are now yours in this one book, to take up and to use, to activate in your own personal life, to transform need and want into prosperity and plenty.

WHAT WILL THESE OCCULT AND MYSTIC POWERS DO FOR YOU?

Anything and everything! Make a wish, express a desire, cite a need—you now have the power to obtain what you want! *Power* will mean the money you want, the luck you need, the love you deserve, the command you require, the health you cherish—and more!

Your 13 Powers will open the doors to a whole new world for you, a secret world emerging from your own mystic center, not from outside where success is often hit or miss. "I turn back into myself," Goethe said, "and discover a world." And what a world it will be when *you* discover it! It is the world of personal power that you will find, the world denied and disparaged by "modern" skeptics and critics This is the world which is discovered by men and women who dare to take up the power of subjective reality, the power not perceptible to the sensory organs, the power behind the visible creation that will give vigor and vitality to your newly empowered life

The 13 Powers available to you here in this book comprise a total package of psychic dynamite that will open up the "other world" of personal power to you. While others struggle for equality, uniformity, and sameness, you will do as the ancient occultists and mystics did: you will emerge *different*, *unique*, *powerful*, *masterful*—an *individual*. The best in life is rarely available to groups, only to individuals. Success, like salvation, happens to *persons*, not people. You will be one of those privileged persons. It is the individual with Power who is creative, fortunate, self-confident, and successful. It is self-determination that brings success, self-determination based on personal, private, potent POWER!

Revealed at last!–You have at your fingertips the accumulation of years of wisdom, secrets, and techniques.

Each secret revealed to you in your *Parker Lifetime Treasury of Mystic and Occult Powers* represents a dynamic success formula or key. In each case the formula is the result of labor performed assiduously by Masters in the field of individual power. *Psychic dynamite* is what you have in your hands right now. This is not merely a book, nor is it for the timid. It is meant for those with the daring and courage of the astronaut, of the inward searcher—for those not afraid to use real power. This is your personal key, your dynamic PROGRAM to a *lifetime* of riches, fame, health, enjoyment, happiness and—last but not least—POWER!

YOU START STORING POWER IMMEDIATELY AND INSTANTANEOUSLY—AND USE IT NOW!

Success and fulfillment need no longer be "sometime in the future," nor need your personal happiness depend on "someone else." With the mystic and occult powers revealed in this easy-to-use program, you will begin to utilize psychic and paranormal forces today!

Others are now doing it. So will you! Here are just some examples of the benefits in store for you:

Steve B. transformed the brink of financial disaster into a high-paying job with the help of the Miracle Mind Magic Stimulator.

Ben and Karen T. went from famine to fame and fortune with the power of Good Luck which they acquired through the use of the secret of Mana-Force.

Hundreds upon hundreds of people are attracting thousands upon thousands of dollars by making themselves living Money Magnets.

J.D. employed the amazing power of Hypno-Cybernetics and rescued his business from disastrous failure.

A Pennsylvania couple turned a drab existence into an exciting, fulfilling life through the use of Psychic Power.

A bedtime amulet ritual gave jobless Harry N. an idea from which he launched his own business, his first sale amounting to $23,000.

Men and women everywhere are activating the magical power of secret spells and are reaping a harvest of personal rewards.

James L. reveals how the power of Psycho-Pictography gets him money, cars, girls—anything and everything he wants or desires.

A loving mother completely cured her ailing boy by applying the secret power of metaphysical healing.

D.J. used the secret of astral travel to get remarkable financial assistance from his departed mother.

New Avatar Power increases success and wealth, joy and happiness virtually overnight.

Gordon was psychically helped to attract the sum of $20,000.

Mrs. Rita L. used Mind Cosmology to renew her love life and to experience new joy and fulfillment.

TO HELP YOU ACTIVATE YOUR DORMANT
POWERS YOU WILL FIND IN THIS BOOK:

Mystic Master Keys: Revelations of Masters in the occult which trigger latent energies needed for your success in life here and now.

True-Life Case Histories: Illustrative examples of people just like yourself who activated their mystic and occult powers to become free, enriched, fulfilled individuals.

Questions and Answers: Questions asked by people before they became happy and successful through the use of their own mystic and occult powers; answers provided will prove beneficial to you in the beginning and invaluable to you later when you review your new Powers.

Occultomatic Power Stimulators: Each chapter contains a do-it-yourself exercise, a concrete action you can take to make each Power your very own. The mystic and occult feedback of each action will empower you to activate in your life exciting and rewarding forces.

Power-Pointers: Each chapter closes with short, powerful reminders which you can check back to for quick and easy memory refreshment about each Power, affording you constant contact with the source of Power.

MAKE THIS TREASURY OF POWERS
YOUR OWN PERPETUAL GUIDE
TO LIFE MORE ABUNDANT

Read with expectation and anticipation. Write out or otherwise mark passages that give you a deep "Aha!" feeling. These are your personal cues to richer, fuller living. Study each Power carefully—adopt it, take it in, absorb it, *treasure* it. The more you think of these Powers as your *own*, the greater will be their positive effect in your personal life.

Now, make the first treasure your own: the secret to unleashing your Mental Power. Be prepared for instant changes in your ability, your circumstances, your very life! This will prepare you for the next dynamic Power. Soon all 13 mystic and occult Powers will be at your beck and call, imbuing your life with wonder-making capabilities, filling every moment with promise, advancement, achievement, and joy! Then your 13 Powers will indeed be your lifetime treasury of prosperity!

Start now to realize: *In thine hand is power* (I Chronicles 29:12).

Theodor Laurence

ACKNOWLEDGMENT

Parker Publishing Company gratefully acknowledges permission to include in the *Parker Lifetime Treasury of Mystic and Occult Powers* chapters and adaptations from the following books:

Buckland & Carrington, *Amazing Secrets of the Psychic World* (West Nyack, NY, Parker Publishing Company, Inc., 1975)

Gray-Cobb, *The Miracle of New Avatar Power*, (West Nyack, NY, Parker Publishing Company, Inc., 1975)

Howard, *Psycho-Pictography: The New Way to Use the Miracle Power of Your Mind* (West Nyack, NY, Parker Publishing Company, Inc., 1965)

Malak, *The Mystic Grimoire of Mighty Spells and Rituals* (West Nyack, NY, Parker Publishing Company, Inc., 1967)

Manning, *The Miracle of Universal Psychic Power*, (West Nyack, NY, Parker Publishing Company, Inc., 1974)

Manning, *Helping Yourself with White Witchcraft*, (West Nyack, NY, Parker Publishing Company, Inc., 1972)

Monahan, *Miracle of Metaphysical Healing* (West Nyack, NY, Parker Publishing Company, Inc., 1975)

Morris, *Miracle of Mana-Force: Secret of Wealth, Love and Power* (West Nyack, NY, Parker Publishing Company, Inc., 1975)

Norvell, *Mind Cosmology* (West Nyack, NY, Parker Publishing Company, Inc., 1971)

Norvell, *Money Magnetism: How to Grow Rich Beyond Your Wildest Dreams* (West Nyack, NY, Parker Publishing Company, Inc., 1974)

Norvell, *The Occult Sciences: How to Get What You Want Through Your Occult Powers* (West Nyack, NY, Parker Publishing Company, Inc., 1971)

Petrie & Stone, *Hypno-Cybernetics: Helping Yourself to a Rich New Life* (West Nyack, NY, Parker Publishing Company, Inc., 1973)

Young, *Secret of Spirit-Thought Magic* (West Nyack, NY, Parker Publishing Company, Inc., 1971)

CONTENTS

The Truth About the Power of Your Brain • "Rest Is Essential" Says This Mystic Master Who Has Helped Thousands to a Better Life • Acquired Mental Distortions That Limit Your Secret Mental Powers and How to Overcome Them • Mystic Master Key • The Three Steps of the Miracle Mind Magic Stimulator to Trigger Your Secret Mental Powers • How to Practice Intensifying the Miracle Mind Magic Stimulator • How Steve B. Obtained a High-Paying Job and Saved Himself and His Family from the Brink of Disaster • Questions and Answers About the Secret of the Power of the Miracle Mind Magic Stimulator • How the Miracle Mind Magic Stimulator Works • Avoid the Most Vicious Vampire of All—Poor Mouthing • Occultomatic Power Stimulator • Power-Pointers

How to Awaken the Fiery Serpent of Psychic Energy and Blaze Your Way to Success • How Bill and Emmy D Turned Their "Average Existence" into an "Amazing Life' • Advanced Study for the Man and Woman of Power • How to Cultivate Your "Sixth Sense" to Help You Help Yourself • Questions and Answers Concerning

the
parker lifetime treasury
of
mystic
and occult powers

POWER 1

how to unleash your secret mental powers

*The Truth About the Power
of Your Brain*

how dare one person tell another that he "can't" succeed or change his life-style or alter his dreadful circumstances? It happens every day!

Sad to say, I have heard this pessimistic note in the voices of clergymen, teachers, lecturers and even in the voices of the parents and loved ones of persons in need of real, concrete aid.

IT IS NOT TRUE! You *can* change your life for the better—here and now! You *will* better your lot in life—if you desire it whole-heartedly. You have probably heard the story of how man uses only one-tenth of his brain, and you have probably heard the exclamation: "Just imagine what we could accomplish if we used our *whole* brain!" Well, I'd like to alter that story just a bit. Ask yourself: "What would happen if I used *two*-tenths of my brain?" Oh, it would be nice to be able to utilize all of one's brain power, but pause and consider the phenomenal things you already accomplish with this denigrated ten percent of brain! Vast strides in progress, world-travel, amazing inventions, love, hope, waking to each new day, life itself—all are possible by the use of only ten percent of our brain power! If all this and more can be accomplished with so little, imagine what you will do with just ten percent more brain power! Let's not be greedy. Let's be satisfied with the fulfillment of our desires, the meeting of your daily needs, the power to survive, and the joy of love and health. All of these things are yours when you unleash your dormant mental powers.

"REST IS ESSENTIAL," SAYS THIS MYSTIC MASTER WHO HAS HELPED THOUSANDS TO A BETTER LIFE

Few of us give a thought to the fact that the very process of thinking—like wishing and hoping—uses mental energy. If our thoughts are idle or even if our energy gets used up at work or play, it is essential that we recuperate before trying occult and mystic techniques. Frank Rudolph Young, "the man of wonder," the internationally esteemed scientist of the mind, has developed *Secret Mental Powers: Miracle of Mind Magic*, an amazing technique for unleashing your latent mental powers, the secret of which is the subject of this chapter. To get *more* brain power, Mr. Young says, you have to take care of the brain power now at your disposal. Why? Because you will be using that most remarkable organ, your brain, to develop your new Powers.

> Brain-work, it is essential to realize, is nearly twice as tiring as manual labor. When you work with your brain you need more sleep and rest than when you work with muscle "alone." It takes only about four hours sleep to restore your physical energy, scientists have proven in the laboratory, but nearly twice as long to recover from brain fatigue . . . It is wisest to be rested before you trigger and use a secret mental power, if you expect the best results for your effort.

Establish yourself in a comfortable position and rest your eyes and brain by relaxing a bit before undertaking the occult and mystic techniques in this book. Rejuvenate yourself, re-charge your "batteries." Once you have rested sufficiently, the next step, according to Mr. Young, is to eradicate in yourself those "mental distortions" that weaken you.

ACQUIRED MENTAL DISTORTIONS THAT
LIMIT YOUR SECRET MENTAL POWERS AND
HOW TO OVERCOME THEM

Your Mental Power is limited to the degree that you feel inferior to others. What makes you feel inferior? Be honest with yourself in order to catch these demons. Different people have different "worries." One man thinks his nose is too large, another believes he is too short, a woman worries about the size of her breasts, another thinks she is "too old" to succeed. "The amount of your income, your lack of importance where you work, the possibility of your not being secure enough in your old age, your diminishing sexual potency, the uncertainties of the stock market, the fidelity of your marriage partner, your children's behavior in school or college, your having to start a new career in middle age"—these are just some of the "demons" Mr. Young lists that will deplete your personal power. Whatever it is that debilitates you—get rid of it! Here's how:

MYSTIC MASTER KEY

Think of something else at once—something you enjoy and which took place already. Think of some sport event, for instance, in which the team or athlete you favored won spectacularly, and relive the contest in your conscious mind. Think of a vacation in which you had a whale of a good time. Think of someone you met whose company you relished no end. Even play solitaire, if you delight in that. "Flee" from the intolerable situation of the present, in other words, by "daydreaming" productively about the past.

Let's now examine the key to your increased Mental Power, Mr. Young's startling secret of the Miracle Mind Magic Stimulator,

which you will use to make yourself as rich, as popular, as successful as you deserve to be!

THE THREE STEPS OF THE MIRACLE MIND
MAGIC STIMULATOR TO TRIGGER YOUR
SECRET MENTAL POWERS

In just three important but easy steps you will induce in your
own brain the Miracle Mind Magic Stimulator. With a little practice
they will become second nature to you and in time will intensify so
they will release your latent Power. Practice them alone in the
privacy of your home and before you know it you will be applying
them easily and surprisingly in your daily life.

Here are the three fantastic steps of the Miracle Mind Magic
Stimulator. Right now, simply read them through, introduce yourself to them, and later you can practice them assiduously and conscientiously.

*Step 1: (a) Think of whatever goal, dream, or wish you want
to come true, for about five seconds.*

*(b) Immediately visualize it as coming true, and main-
tain that vision for about four seconds.*

*Step 2: (a) Think of that goal, dream, or wish again for about
five seconds. But this time dig deep into your conscious mind for it and drag out its details.*

*(b) Immediately visualize it again as coming true, and
maintain that vision for about four seconds. But,
visualize it far more clearly and completely than
before. Let the details fit into it, as if it were
actually occurring.*

*Step 3: (a) Once more think of that goal, dream, or wish, for
about five seconds. But this time dig so deeply into
your mind for it that you extract every possible
detail about it.*

> (b) *Immediately visualize it once more as coming true, and maintain that vision for about four seconds. But, visualize it so thoroughly in every detail that it seems to "come true" right before your eyes.*

These three simple steps are very similar to techniques used by Ancient Masters and they are your key to a Mystic Power that will amaze you.

HOW TO PRACTICE INTENSIFYING THE MIRACLE MIND MAGIC STIMULATOR

What exactly is it you want? More money? A mate? Bread on the table? A pay raise? Perhaps you need more love in your life. Maybe you need a loved one healed of some terrible affliction or trouble.

Whatever you want, need or desire, this Mystic Power is yours to use and to create miracles in your own life. Practice it daily if possible—first rest from your labors and then go through the three easy steps. Practice diligently, every opportunity you get. Visualize with intense clarity your dream, wish or desire. Don't be afraid to take more time than the exercise calls for, if you require more time. The important thing in the beginning is to learn this mystic technique until it is part of you. In time you can reduce the time span to that called for. What remains vital at all times is your complete interest and focus on your vision of dream, goal or wish. In your mind's eye examine it closely, explore its every detail, as if you were trying to memorize it. What will result is that your accurately visualized dream or goal will *attract* your latent Mental Power. The latter will imbue the former; the Mystic Power will trigger your hope or wish, activating it on the physical plane. In short, your dream will come true!

If your dream, hope or need is transportation, for instance, visualize an automobile, as in the above first step, as already true.

See yourself obtaining a car! Don't see yourself *wishing* for the car—you already have it! See yourself in your mind's eye *driving* that needed automobile! You can count on this Mystic Power as developed by Mr. Young. I have seen this power of visualization work in many lives.

HOW STEVE B. OBTAINED A HIGH-PAYING JOB AND SAVED HIMSELF AND HIS FAMILY FROM THE BRINK OF DISASTER

Steve B. of Canton, Ohio, was in the same boat as many other jobless men: his bills were due and mounting; his young wife and small children were practically on a starvation diet; a finance company threatened to repossess his car; and, worst of all, Steve was drinking too much, trying to drown his troubles. Steve began to associate with some tavern rowdies and copied their example, complaining about everything: prices, inequities, the rich getting richer and the poor getting poorer, and a host of other "reasons" for his failure in life.

But that was before he learned of the Miracle Mind Magic Stimulator. It was on a Friday afternoon that Steve began practicing the three steps outlined above. On the following Monday he was the Assistant Office Manager of a big corporation, salaried at $800 a month. How did this miracle occur?

Strangely enough, it began when Steve was staggering home; he toppled off a curb and fell into the street, narrowly missing getting hit by a car. The car's driver slammed on the brakes just in time and emerged shaken and perspiring, thinking he had actually hit the unfortunate man. Mr. James L. was greatly relieved to see that Steve had suffered no more than a scratch on the arm. Mr. L. helped Steve to his feet and insisted on driving him home.

Here he met Steve's delightful family, his pretty wife Anna and his two children—Tom, aged four, and Lisa, aged two. Mr. L., a man sensitive to human tragedy, sounded both of them out after Anna invited him to stay for tea (coffee was too expensive for them). While Steve slowly sobered up, Mr. L. listened to this family's woes. It was heart-rending, but Mr. L. knew he was in no position to help them materially. But he knew about the Magic Mind Stimulator; it had helped him. Wouldn't it help Steve, too?

For the next hour and a half Mr. L. explained the function of the Stimulator to Anna and Steve. Steve, however, was hardly in a condition to listen and absorb. But Anna was.

That evening, while Steve "slept it off," Anna rested in the living room. She was following the three easy steps outlined above. Friday night, Saturday morning, Saturday afternoon, during the childrens' naps, Sunday morning after church, Sunday afternoon—Anna B. was practicing, practicing, practicing. Her efforts were rewarded in a miraculous way.

On Monday morning they received a call from Mr. L. What, he wanted to know, did Steve do for a living when he was working? Anna said Steve was really versatile and usually dependable (only worried and under stress right now) and that he could do almost anything. Could he type, for instance, Mr. L. asked. Yes, he could. Has he had any managerial experience? Yes, said Anna, Steve had been the foreman in a factory for over three years.

"Fine!" Mr. L. erupted into the phone. "Send him over here right away, in a business suit. My Assistant Manager has left me in the lurch and I need help fast."

Anna almost fainted with joy and incredulity. "But that's uncanny!" she emoted.

"What is?"

"Well, remember that Mind Stimulator you were telling us about? I've been doing it since you left. But this is the uncanny part: I was visualizing Steve in a business suit in a nice clean office, making lots of money without having to slave for it!"

Mr. L. chuckled over the phone and exclaimed, "No wonder my Assistant Manager disappeared!"

Not only does Steve no longer drink and complain; he drinks coffee brewed by a very happy wife and smiling children.

Moreover, when Anna told him what she had done, Steve was then eager to learn about the mystic technique for altering circumstances. Now he's practicing the three magic steps. Why? This ambitious young man wants a promotion into a *higher* paying position in the company!

You set your own limits with the Miracle Mind Magic Stimulator!

QUESTIONS AND ANSWERS ABOUT THE SECRET OF THE POWER OF THE MIRACLE MIND MAGIC STIMULATOR

Question: Is it right for a person to want riches?
Answer: Not only is it right, it is self-defeatism to settle for less! You know your full worth and you should not be satisfied with less.

Question: What's the best way of using this technique for getting a marriage partner?
Answer: Mr. Young's suggestion that you visualize *in detail* brings up an interesting point. When visualizing a man or a woman always add to your mental picture, *in detail*, the *qualities* you wish your new mate to have, not only his or her physical characteristics. You don't want a bad product in an attractive package!

Question: How can I get the one I love to say "Yes" to marriage?
Answer: It is always a temptation to nag, inveigle or trick a mate into a positive response. Don't do it. If you will use the Miracle Mind Magic Stimulator as directed you will be amazed to find your loved one coming to you with the proposal. Strongly visualize him or her actually asking *you* the big question: "Will you marry me?"

Question: A local store in my neighborhood has a weekly drawing for groceries and money. Can the Miracle Mind Magic Stimulator help me win?
Answer: That's a very good test for this Power. Follow the instructions to the letter. Get alone with yourself. Relax. Close your eyes. And visualize yourself being contacted by the store manager to say you are the winner this week. Concentrate on every detail: see

yourself answering the phone, being informed of your good fortune, excitedly donning a coat, leaving the house, hurrying to the store, and, most of all, reaching out your hand for the grand prize! This same procedure is good where any sweepstakes are concerned. A woman in Toledo who had only fifty dollars to her name won a contest and received $5000!

HOW THE MIRACLE MIND MAGIC STIMULATOR WORKS

With the Miracle Mind Magic Stimulator, you bring together the requisite psychic energies which are needed to alter your brain patterns, and create the proper milieu in which to trigger the right secret mental power you need for your goal, dream, or wish. Your normal brain capacity of ten percent efficiency is not strong enough to bring about the stimulation of psychic centers needed. Your acquired lack of success restrains your mind from flashing the charge of energy required to bring about miracles in your life. With the three-step Stimulator, however, the vividness of your vision of success which you create for your goal, dream, or wish is so *savagely real* that your whole body responds to it as if that vision had already come true, and actually *changes* the circumstances preventing your complete happiness. Consequently, success is yours!

This is why you *must create* the Miracle Mind Magic Stimulator in three steps. Each step multiplies the seeming reality of the previous one, until your final vision in Step 3 seems so real to you that it *compels* your brain to exert its secret forces. This immediately transforms your luck.

AVOID THE MOST VICIOUS VAMPIRE OF ALL—"POOR MOUTHING"

Resist saying, "I don't even have enough money to purchase food stamps."

Visualize: A truckload of food, a *freightcar* load of food. Of course, you don't want a freightcar load of food, but this exaggerated visualization will send the proper message to your subconscious mind. Think BIG when you visualize!

Don't lament, "I don't have a car."

Visualize: You've just won a contest—a brand new Super car! It's yours, free! See the color, the lines, the design, the beauty! See yourself driving it!

Don't cry, "He (or she) doesn't love me!"

Visualize: The greatest, most enduring love you have ever known is now yours! How fortunate you are!

Stop listing your "Don't have's" and start listing your "have's." Visualize them, employ the three easy steps of the Miracle Mind Magic Stimulator, imagine yourself already in possession of those things you so desperately want and need. Don't let that negative attitude of "I don't have" dictate your reality. Change that reality NOW!

OCCULTOMATIC POWER STIMULATOR

The following questions are representative of the major desires that brighten everyone's life. How would you answer them? Write out your answers. Then visualize intensely whatever picture comes to your mind with each question and answer.

1. *If I could have a change of residence, what would I like my new home to look like?*

2. *What would I like to have most right now?*

3. *How do I see "the good life"?*

4. *What do we need to make our lives happier: more money, a vacation, a relaxing trip, a new television set?*

5. *Of my needs, what is first on the list? Second?*

6. *What can I do right now to supplement my Mystic Power?*

7. *What kind of a job would I like to hold?*

8. *If I were self-employed and self-sufficient, in what field would I excel?*

9. *What is the minimum amount of money I need to achieve my goals?*

10. *How can I improve life for my family and loved ones?*

POWER-POINTERS

Permit *no one* to tell you that you "can't" succeed or change your life. Reject all such pessimistic advice, and go forth conquering! Mystic Power helps you to gain those joys of life you richly deserve.

REST IS ESSENTIAL. Relax in a pleasant chair or sofa or even on a bed. Close your eyes for a few moments. Slow your breathing down. Inhale deeply, slowly, smoothly. Recuperate from your labors of this day before you apply the secrets of occult and mystic techniques. You will need all the brain power at your disposal.

Beware of those worries and depressions that can sap your vital energy. Set them aside for now by thinking of something else immediately, something pleasant, pleasurable, some remembered success or victory or good time. But get away from today's troubles as you activate your Mystic Power.

Practice the three steps of visualization as outlined for you. Take each step separately and apply it to your daily life with diligence. Set your goal firmly in your mind and then carry it with concentration through the three magic steps to success.

Remember that Steve B. was on the brink of disaster and yet almost overnight realized success and happiness in his own life and in the lives of those around him. You can do the same!

The Miracle Mind Magic Stimulator is your first Power in the growing arsenal of your treasure house. Use this easy three-step process with your every visualization—and watch your dreams come true!

Avoid "poor mouthing" and counting up your troubles. Think positive, believe big, hope ceaselessly, and reap a harvest of riches!

Editor's Note on Power #1:

You may have already been using this Power without realizing it. Many of us idly imagine or visualize things. But now you are to make this process of visualization an *action*. No more idle "woolgathering," but active, progressive, creative imagination! Record your visualizations in a notebook and keep it where you can review it from time to time. Check what you write against the sections of this chapter. Make this a creative habit and do it with all the chapters.

This is your personal Treasury of Occult and Mystic Powers, but do not write or mark on the book as this will diminish the powers. Instead, transfer important passages, instructions, directions, case histories or keys that have special meaning for you to your personal Study Book (any inexpensive notebook will suffice for this purpose).

This practice will impress your subconscious mind with the tips and keys you are receiving from this book's occult and mystic Masters.

The next Power comes to you from two psychic researchers who have achieved astounding results in their own lives with the Power they will share with you. Today they enjoy health, wealth and success. You will enjoy the same benefits when you study, absorb, and assimilate the secret psychic knowledge they now reveal.

POWER 2

the amazing secret of psychic power revealed

*How to Awaken the Fiery Serpent
of Psychic Energy and
Blaze Your Way to Success . . .*

$t$he magical results of Power #2 are reserved for those who have diligently studied and *practiced* the first Power. Through this study and practice you begin to transcend the limitations of ten-percent brain power and you release additional energy. What will you do with this increased supply of vital force? You will learn how to channel it into constructive and creative outlets *for your own benefit*. The energy released by Power #1 will be transformed into Power #2: PSYCHIC POWER!

HOW BILL AND EMMY D. TURNED THEIR "AVERAGE EXISTENCE" INTO AN "AMAZING LIFE"

Bill and Emmy D. of Scranton, Pennsylvania, both in their early twenties were, like so many of their contemporaries, living "hand to mouth," just making ends meet. In fact, there were many days, say this couple, when "ends" never met at all. But that was before they switched from "traditional" ways of doing things to the use of occult and mystic Powers.

Bill and Emmy undertook to develop their own psychic powers, to invite the aid of "the other world." At a lecture they attended one evening they heard a psychic investigator say: "You don't have to be poor! Show me a poor person and I will show you a person who doesn't know his own psychic potential!"

Bill and Emmy decided to change their attitude toward psychic things and determined to be rich. For four years Bill had been selling vacuum cleaners door-to-door. For a while he drove a taxi. Both jobs were unfulfilling and unrewarding. He sincerely and urgently wanted a change in his life. What neither he nor Emmy knew as they sat in the audience was that their combined aura of expectancy and undiminished hope was actually projecting through the room. They did not know of such things on this first evening. But they soon learned.

The lecturer suddenly stopped in the middle of his dissertation. His eyes scanned the room like radar beams. They settled on Bill and Emmy. After a few seconds pause, he resumed his lecture, but immediately after its end, he called to Bill and Emmy and asked them to accompany him into his office. He got right to the point.

"You two are in need of help," he said bluntly, amazing Bill and Emmy. "I could feel your essence clear across the room." He turned to Bill and said, "You have been working hard and receiving little in return for your devotion and effort. We're going to change all that. Sit down, please. And listen to me."

Bill and Emmy listened rapt, dumbfounded, as this stranger "read" their lives as if he had known them for years. He seemed to know their hopes and desires, their frustrations and setbacks. And he proceeded to instruct them in the power and use of secret mental forces.

Less than a week later the life of Bill and Emmy began to change in a most miraculous manner. A distant relative of Emmy's passed away and left her the sum of $5,000. But this was only the beginning. Employing their newfound "sixth sense," Bill and Emmy bought into a small company. Their partner said he'd sell them his interest for an additional $15,000. As Bill and Emmy walked home that evening, thinking of the great opportunity to own their own business, they bumped into an old friend whom they hadn't seen in years. Apparently he had made it big in oil. Bill felt a stirring in his solar plexus, a "prodding" of the sixth sense. No sooner had they said hello when Bill burst out: "How would you like to make $20,000? Lend me $15,000 right now and I guarantee to pay you back $20,000."

The oil man couldn't resist. "There was something about them," he said later to a newspaperman. "As we stood there in the street I just knew I *had* to lend Bill the money."

Bill and Emmy bought their company. Today that company—now a vast corporation—is worth millions of dollars.

In their luxurious California home, next to their two-car garage occupied by a Mercedes Benz and a Cadillac, Bill and Emmy attest: "It's psychic power. Money is fine, but if you know how to mix psychic energy with it, money just multiplies like rabbits!"

ADVANCED STUDY FOR THE MAN
AND WOMAN OF POWER

You, too, can see your life change miraculously! Prepare yourself by practicing Power #1. Then get ready to assimilate the magic of Power #2. This advanced study is suitable only for those aspirants who have developed a certain amount of mastery of the inner self, who have succeeded in attaining Power.

Progress—which may be slow, and consequently somewhat frustrating at times—is necessary in psychic development as in every other field of endeavor, and those who have gone this far should advance their powers and faculties yet another step forward into that vast and mystic beyond which encircles us on every side.

HOW TO CULTIVATE YOUR "SIXTH SENSE"
TO HELP YOU HELP YOURSELF

Raymond Buckland and Hereward Carrington, the two psychic investigators who have revealed the secret of your "Seven Vital Centers," in *Amazing Secrets of the Psychic World* point out your first step in releasing your inner powers is to cultivate as far as possible your sixth sense. The five traditional senses of sight, smell, taste, hearing, and touching have stood you in good stead all of your life; it is this additional sixth sense that can create miracles in your life.

QUESTIONS AND ANSWERS CONCERNING MIRACLE-WORKING BY YOUR NEW PSYCHIC POWER

The following questions asked by people just like yourself are answered by Buckland and Carrington. Examine each carefully and learn from them.

Question: What is the sixth sense?
Answer: This sixth sense is a general feeling of "awareness" of surrounding powers and entities—a knowledge which is not dependent on any of the five senses.

Question: How can I develop my sixth sense?
Answer: Breathing is of vital importance in cultivating your extrasensory faculties. A certain number of breathing exercises should be taken daily.

Question: Why is breathing so important?
Answer: There is a peculiar life-giving property in fresh air, and if we do not breathe this fully we never *live* as completely and receive as large a supply of the vital currents of the universe as we otherwise would. If anyone doubts this he has but to stand erect and do half a dozen deep breathing exercises, as directed below, and he will feel energized from head to toe. The way to do these exercises so as to get the best results is as follows:

MASTER MYSTIC KEY

1. Standing before an open window, free from all restrictive clothing. Before beginning, exhale forcibly, bending the body forward and relaxing the muscles. Place both open hands over the abdomen. Now breathe as deeply as possible against these hands, expanding the abdomen as much as possible without allowing the chest or ribs to expand in the least. In other words, breathe with the abdomen only.

2. *After you have done this five or six times place both your hands against your ribs on either side. Now breathe in deeply, pressing out the ribs, but without allowing either the abdomen or the upper chest to expand.*

3. *After you have done this five or six times place your hands on the upper chest, just below the neck, and breathe with this portion of the lungs without allowing either the ribs or the abdomen to expand.*

THERE IS MORE TO YOUR BREATHING THAN YOU THINK

To most of us breathing is simply inhaling and exhaling. To the Ancient Masters, however, it is infinitely more. In fact, they do not speak of "breathing" at all; they speak of "*prana*," which includes the psychic aspect of human breathing.

HOW TO DEVELOP YOUR PSYCHIC BREATHING AND CONTROL THE MAGIC OF PRANA

Study this section of your second Power carefully. Write down the instructions to make them a part of your very being. By all means, *practice* this breathing technique in order to evoke your own psychic Power.

1 *Breathe rhythmically until the rhythm is perfectly established.*

2 *While inhaling and exhaling in this rhythmic fashion, form the mental image of your breath being drawn up through the bones of your legs; then through the bones of your arms;*

then the top of your skull; then through your stomach; then through your reproductive region; then as if it were traveling up and down along your spinal column.

3. *Now form the mental image of your breath being inhaled and exhaled through the pores of your skin.*

HOW TO AWAKEN YOUR "CHAKRAS" OR SEVEN VITAL CENTERS

By practicing the above breathing technique you are teaching yourself the rudiments of controlling *prana*, a magical force lying dormant in your being. Practice often and conscientiously. Get familiar with your breathing. Then you are ready to employ your new knowledge in a *psychic* way. Once you become adept at "mentally" directing your breath through your bones, as it were, you are prepared to direct *prana* through your "Seven Vital Centers," which will activate them.

Here is the next step in your program of self-development which leads you to new and glorious success and happiness:

Form a mental image of your prana-breath and, inhaling and exhaling slowly, send it to:

1. *The very end of your spinal column.*

2. *To your reproductive region.*

3. *To your solar plexus.*

4. *To your heart.*

5. *To your throat.*

6. *To a spot between your eyes.*

7. *To a spot at the very top of your brain.*

These seven vital centers of the body are known as *chakras* and have very great importance in all higher psychic development and in all occult practice, say Buckland and Carrington.

It is upon the awakening of the Seven Centers, in fact, that all the higher clairvoyance and psychical faculties depend. They are supposed to be the links of connection between the physical and the astral bodies.

THE PSYCHIC WAY TO SET YOUR GOALS AND ACHIEVE THEM

As you practice the above breathing and *prana* exercises, keep in mind why you are undertaking this regimen. You are learning these occult and mystic secrets in order to change your life. You want more money, more fun out of life, a smiling face, beauty, personality, success!

In between sessions of exercise and *prana*-control,

1. *Write down your goal, dream or wish. Keep the list of the things you want out of life beside you as you cultivate your chakras.*

2. *Write your wishes out in clear language. Like Bill and Emmy D., you will realize your dreams.*

3. *Think BIG! If you need money, for example, ask not for ten dollars (or that is all you will get!), but ask for a hundred dollars, a thousand, ten thousand! Riches will accumulate to you in direct proportion that your sixth sense transmits its desire.*

4. *Practice this Buckland-Carrington way to prana control. Much depends upon your awakening of your Seven Vital Centers!*

HOW TO ENLIST THE MAGICAL AID OF THE "FIERY SERPENT" THAT LIES COILED UP IN YOUR MYSTIC CENTER

The Vital Energy which passes upwards through your seven *chakras* is symbolized as a Fiery Serpent which, in passing upward, animates each in turn and wakes them into activity. It is highly important that this current of energy should pass through each center in the *right order*—from the end of your spinal cord to the top of your head.

In Sanskrit, the Fiery Serpent is called *Kundalini*. This serpent-energy leads not only to the awakening of the higher psychical faculties, but exerts an influence on your very life and being. Once you awaken this powerful ally, it will come into play in your mentally imaged wishes, dreams and goals. With practice you will then be able to call it up at will.

When you feel you have become proficient at controlling your breathing physically and your *prana* psychically, you will be free to evoke your Fiery Serpent at any time, by using the following simple device:

OCCULTOMATIC POWER STIMULATOR

Sit straight, and look at the tip of your nose. By controlling the two optic nerves one advances a long way towards the control of the arc of reaction, and so to the control of the will. Imagine a lotus upon the top of the head, several inches up, and Virtue as its center, the stalk as knowledge. The eight petals of the lotus are the eight powers of the Yogi. Inside of the lotus think of the Golden One, the Almighty, the Intangible. Think of a space in your heart, and in the midst of that space think of a fire burning. Think of that flame in your own Soul, and inside this flame is another space, effulgent, and that is the soul of your soul—God.

When you have advanced in study and practice you will be able to summon Kundalini to help you by pronouncing the sacred word OM. Say it now to get familiar with it. Draw the word out, like this:

OOOOOOOOOOMMMMMMMMMMM . . .

When pronouncing the "M" let your lips vibrate. Let the sound of OM vibrate throughout your entire body. Feel it. Pronounce it again. And again. And again. In time you will be able to pronounce mentally and achieve the same miraculous, shape-shifting, wonder-working Power.

WHAT CAN YOU EXPECT FROM YOUR NEW PSYCHIC POWER

Different people who have developed their occult and mystic Powers use them in different ways. Once you have developed them they can be used in any of a variety of ways. Perhaps you can use some extra money. Let your Seven Vital Centers aid you. Maybe you need more love or compassion or sympathy. Let your Fiery Serpent loose! Are enemies plaguing you, interfering in your private life? Set the Serpent on them! Want to hear wedding bells? Activate your Heart Chakra!

To desire is human. Your new psychic power will help you to realize whatever you want, need or wish. Here are the ten basic motives which inspire all human action:

The desire for SELF-SURVIVAL
The desire for LOVE
The desire for SEX
The desire for FREEDOM FROM FEAR
The desire for IMMORTALITY
The desire for SELF-DETERMINATION
The desire for PROTECTION AGAINST EVIL
The desire for POPULARITY AND FAME
The desire for SELF-EXPRESSION AND SUCCESS
The desire for INCREASED WEALTH

When you know the secret to psychic Power and how to activate your Seven Chakras, you know principles which can create miracles in your life.

List your goals, your dreams, your desires, and keep the list handy as you continue to practice your breathing and *prana* exercises. Be patient. Be diligent. Be conscientious. Develop the Powers of your sixth sense first. Occult investigators Buckland and Carrington reveal some of the results you can expect from using your new psychic Power.

SEEING WITH ANY PART OF YOUR BODY
CAN GREATLY FACILITATE YOUR SUCCESS

Just imagine how fortunate you would be if you could "sense" danger before it strikes you! How would you like to be able to "detect" upcoming profit-making opportunities? Wouldn't it be grand if you could "see" ahead?

This amazing kind of "vision" comes with the practice of the exercises laid out for you in this dynamic chapter. It is as though eyes were situated at any point at which you concentrate your forces. "This power," says Buckland and Carrington, "has been cultivated to an extraordinary extent by some of the Eastern Adepts and is recorded as happening spontaneously occasionally, even now, in the East."

Now this amazing faculty is being cultivated here in the West. "There have been recent reports of Russian experimentation in 'seeing with the fingertips.' Here various subjects have been able to distinguish different colored spots on white cards, purely by touch." Now you, too, can benefit materially by this new knowledge.

The power is cultivated by an effort of attention, coupled by will, and should be preceded by the practice of traveling around the body in thought and then holding yourself consciously on one particular point in your circuit of the body, and concentrating yourself on that point.

You can now practice this exercise easily, for you have already (hopefully!) been practicing the "following of your *prana*" exercise.

Now you will focus your attention on a particular section of your anatomy—only in a psychic manner. Let's say, for instance, that you desire Love. Focus your attention upon your Heart after doing the requisite breathing exercises. Form a mental image of the man or woman of your choice while concentrating your energy focus upon your Heart. You will be emanating vibrations into the universe corresponding with your desire for Love and the Law of Karmic Return will then activate to influence your Love object to feel drawn to you. In a similar manner your new psychic Power may be used for achieving popularity, obtaining wealth, developing better health, etc.

All of these exercises should be taken very seriously indeed. They are all designed to bring you access to occult and mystic Powers, which in turn are to be used for the fulfillment of your desires. Follow all instructions carefully and you will be more than pleased with the remarkable results.

HOW TO MAKE YOUR ASTRAL BODY
WORK MIRACLES FOR YOU

At this stage of your development you may begin to practice an exercise which will be of great benefit not only to yourself but to others as well.

Follow these easy instructions:

1. *Do the 3-step breathing exercises.*
2. *Do the 3-step prana exercises.*
3. *Awaken your Seven Vital Centers as directed above.*
4. *Activate your Fiery Serpent.*
5. *Concentrate on one single goal, dream or wish.*
6. *Perform the OCCULTOMATIC POWER STIMULATOR.*
7. *Pronounce OM a few times to set up the proper vibrations.*
8. *Open all the "eyes" of your total body.*
9. *Sit or lie down in a comfortable position. Relax. Think of your astral body, the invisible body that looses itself from your physical body when you are sleeping.*

10. *Now send your astral body to influence those you wish to contact—living or dead. Let your astral body do the work! It can influence others to help you; it can draw loved ones to you; it can repel enemies and threatening people.*

You may, after a certain amount of effort, thus project the astral body and cause it to retain full self-consciousness. When this has been acquired this projected body can assist those who have recently died, confronting them and consoling them, and can carry messages from such a person to those still living. It can assist those in danger, and help along humanity in a thousand different ways. When you have learned to project your astral body in this manner you are known as one of the "Invisible Helpers," and many persons are said to make it a business to perform at least one good action during each exercise.

A WORD OF WARNING ABOUT YOUR NEWLY ACQUIRED OCCULT AND MYSTIC POWERS

You are developing outstanding Powers, and this book is designed to help you do exactly that. It is your own personal Prosperity Program for a richer, happier, more relaxed future. I personally would like you to have your every wish, dream and goal come true. You should be well-fed, smiling, buoyant, vivacious, sparkling, carefree, and deliriously happy. But there are some things I think you should know:

Do use your occult and mystic Powers to make yourself and your loved ones happier.

Do not employ these potent Powers against anyone unless you know beyond a shadow of a doubt that he or she deserves opposition.

Do use your Powers to fatten your bank account.

Do not lust for gold greedily; take only what you need.

Do enjoy life more fully through the use of your new Powers—and make others as happy as yourself!

OCCULT AND MYSTIC POWERS AS TRANSCENDENTAL FORCES IN A TECHNOLOGICAL ENVIRONMENT

Responsibility comes with power. What you are learning is not only how to use occult and mystic Powers, but also how to use them *wisely*. Such gifts are always given to those who will share them, help others, spread the joy. You will find that your sixth sense exercises are in fact spiritual exercises.

Two remarkable psychic manifestations will result from these spiritual practices, if correctly and carefully performed. The first is the enlargement of the Self until it attains a vast area, so to speak, which has been called "Cosmic Consciousness" by those who have experienced it. This consciousness is a step higher than human consciousness and enables us to perceive truth and spiritual reality behind the universe, in addition to stimulating remarkable psychic powers. Such realities as the "fourth dimension," which are usually quite incapable of being appreciated by our finite senses, are said to be clear and intelligible to those who possess Cosmic Consciousness, and the connection between spirit and matter is also clear to them.

YOUR NEW POWER OVER ANIMATE AND INANIMATE MATTER

The second remarkable development from the awakening of these higher spiritual faculties will be the greater power you possess over animate and inanimate nature. You will find that you exert a peculiar influence over all animals with whom you come into contact. They not only seem to know and understand you but, if the animals are wild, they will not harm you in any way.

HOW OCCULT AND MYSTIC POWERS MAKE
YOU A DANIEL IN A LIONS' DEN

As you now affect animals, you will affect people. This means that by using your new Powers with wisdom and circumspection you can influence people to help you, to come to your assistance, to help your loved ones. Moreover, you will be able to ward off danger, threats, setbacks, evil influences and dangerous people. Even if you are surrounded by evil and enmity, like Daniel in his lions' den, you will emerge unscrathed when you use your occult and mystic powers properly.

But this isn't all you can do!

CREATION BY THE POWER YOU
NOW POSSESS

Finally you will be able actually to *create* by the power of your thought. In other words, you will have learned to "create" by the power of the will, and this is one of the greatest achievements gained by the advanced student of the occult.

Nothing can be denied you!

Simply take your occult and mystic exercises seriously. And leave the rest to Powers beyond the human!

POWER-POINTERS

The excess energy released by Power #1 is transformed into Power #2: PSYCHIC POWER!

Advanced study for the man and woman of Power means mastery of the inner Self.

The sixth sense is cultivated through the practice of certain breathing exercises.

The psychic aspect of human breathing is *prana*.

Through breathing and *prana* exercises the Seven Vital Centers or Chakras are awakened.

The Fiery Serpent is Energy!

The practice of exercises coupled with mental images of desires, dreams, and goals makes wishes come true!

Remember the ten basic desires: SELF-SURVIVAL, LOVE, SEX, FREEDOM FROM FEAR, IMMORTALITY, SELF-DETERMINATION, PROTECTION FROM EVIL, POPULARITY AND FAME, SELF-EXPRESSION AND SUCCESS, INCREASED WEALTH. You can fulfill them all!

List your goals, dreams, and desires—and go after them with Power!

Employ the mystic help of your Astral Body.

Always remember to use your new Powers wisely and never negatively.

You have attained Power over animate and inanimate objects. As animals will love and serve you, so will humans.

Editor's Note on Power #2

Bearing in mind all you have learned so far, take a look around you and observe the ways in which people generally *lack* Power. Notice the negative reactions to life's setbacks and trials. When you find yourself about to respond as other people do—STOP!—and review the first two chapters of this book. You need no longer suffer lack and deprivation!

Think of the biggest problem in your life right now. Write down the ways you have already tried to handle this problem. Now do the exercises in this chapter and project your Astral Body to help you. Be ready to record the amazing results!

As you did with your first Power, record any section of this chapter which has special meaning for you. Focus on this and magnify it in your being. You are beginning to use the wonderful Powers which are rightfully yours.

The next Power gives you the occult key to a remarkable means for acquiring wealth: MONEY MAGNETISM. You will learn to use the Power that draws money to you as a magnet draws iron filings, as one sex attracts the other, as gravitation attracts all!

POWER 3

how to pyramid wealth with mystic money power

How To Build Money Magnetism

money can be yours! Never doubt it! If you are one of those people who have suffered lack and deprivation, you will know the value of money. You should not only *need* money; you should *have* all you require! That's easy to say, but how to obtain the money you need? This is the question.

Of primary importance is your belief in the availability of money, which means the end of the defeating thought that there just isn't enough money to go around.

We tend to let circumstances dictate to us. We see lack, hear of lack, and subsequently *believe* in lack. Then we experience lack. But even as we experience lack, the source of riches and plenty is still intact, still overflowing, seeking an outlet. You can be that outlet. As you go about your daily life, *believe* you are in the presence of the wealth-source. Rechannel your power of belief and believe that the Giver of All is right here with you, knows your needs, wishes you well, and delights in supplying you with whatever you want. First and foremost, reactivate your power of belief.

THE QUICKEST AND EASIEST WAY
TO ATTRACT MONEY

Your teacher of Money Power is Norvell who for many years was the advisor of movie stars and industrial magnates and who has also guided many thousands of ordinary men and women to great achievements and resounding financial success.

"One of the quickest ways for you to build money magnetism," says this money Master, "is to associate with people who have already used the power of magnetism to become rich."

Wherever you live, whatever your circumstances, there are people around you who have proven themselves successful in their respective fields. Success formulas have worked miracles in their lives. You can do the same!

By studying, practicing, and developing Power 1 and 2, you prepare yourself for the benefits of Power #3: Money Power! Your practice and study sessions make a veritable Money Magnet of you! When you are in the presence of others who have already achieved success you will profit by listening to them, by taking their advice, by acting upon their suggestions. But, most importantly, as Norvell points out, "you can magnetize their minds with your own projections of thoughts that will endear them to you and make them want to help you." And who doesn't need the help of wealthy people?

You will be amazed by the new properties of your mind after developing the occult and mystic Powers in your *Parker Lifetime Treasury*. As the farmer tills his ground, so Power #1 tills your brain. As the farmer sows his seed, so Power #2 sows potency in your mind. And as the farmer reaps a rich and wholesome crop, so Power #3 makes it possible for you to reap a harvest of riches!

Norvell in his book, *Money Magnetism*, says the quickest way to accumulate money is to bring yourself in contact with people who have money. Here is his 10-point plan for getting the wealth you need.

10 WAYS TO MEET WEALTHY AND PROMINENT PEOPLE

1. One of the easiest ways for you to meet wealthy and important people is to go where such people congregate. It is almost impossible to casually run into such people, but they do go to certain places where you can accidentally cross their paths.

Choose a church where there are regular social events scheduled for the parishioners and attend it every week until you become a regular part of the scene. Then when there are social events, charitable, money-raising bazaars, or other church functions, you will automatically become a part of the scene. In this way you will meet and mingle with outstanding citizens of your community. Soon you will be invited to the homes of prominent people and such contacts will eventually lead to some kind of business or financial involvement.

A young man and his wife came to our lectures in Los Angeles, and they were eager to move into higher circles socially and for business reasons. The young man was a beginning attorney and they were anxious to start building their lives on a solid social foundation.

They followed my advice to join a church of their faith in the wealthy Beverly Hills district. Soon they were making contacts with other church members, some of whom were very important in the business community. One of these contacts was with a judge and his wife. They found the young couple charming and invited them to a small dinner party at their home. It was at this party that the young attorney met a man who was prominent in city government. Later when he needed an assistant in his office, he just naturally chose the young attorney he had met socially! From this beginning this young attorney went on to become an outstanding lawyer, and later ran successfully for public office, backed by the judge and his former employer. He won out over his competition by a wide margin. This was the beginning of a great career for this young man and his wife

2. One of the easiest places for you to meet wealthy and important people is through a social club. This can be an athletic club, a golf or tennis club, or a country club, where socially prominent people gather regularly. It may cost a little to join such a social club but when you once gain acceptance among such people, you will have many invitations and business contacts that will more than repay you for your investment.

A young real estate salesman took my advice once to join the Beverly Hills Hotel Swimming Club. For a small yearly sum he and his wife had a poolside cabana, where they could meet with and entertain their friends all summer. Some of the people they met at the pool were wealthy people who were coming to California to live and they were in the market for houses or apartments.

Soon this real estate salesman was making more sales than anyone in his office. Within two years he opened his own real estate office in Beverly Hills and had 10 salesmen working for him. He was soon making friends among prominent businessmen and social-ites, and his business operation became enormously successful, giv-ing him security and prominence in his community.

3. To gain admittance to the offices of prominent and wealthy businessmen, write letters to 10 of the outstanding businessmen in your community, offering them ideas and suggestions for their busi-ness. Place no price tag on such ideas, but give them freely. If they are good ideas you will be given an interview and an opportunity of presenting them in person. After you have made these contacts you can later write letters to them asking if there are any openings in their organizations for your particular talents.

A young man just out of college wanted to get into advertising, but he had no contacts in that field. He learned these techniques for meeting important people by attending some of my lectures in New York City. He prepared an elaborate scrapbook in which he mounted all the important advertisements appearing in current periodicals and newspapers for cigarettes, cosmetics, household appliances, television sets, automobiles, food products and liquor ads. Then on each page he added his suggestions of how these ads could be improved so as to sell more products.

One particular firm that he approached happened to handle one of the products he had put into his scrapbook. It was a drug product. The advertising company used his suggestion for a television com-mercial, which instantly doubled the sale of the product! From that beginning this young man was given a job with one of the biggest advertising agencies in the city and a bonus of $10,000 for his new idea for a TV commercial!

4. To get into the higher brackets of social or business activ-ities, make it a point to offer your services to any lodge or

charitable group that is doing something for the good of the community or a particular charity, such as Lighthouse for the Blind, American Cancer Society, Multiple Sclerosis, Heart Fund, Jewish Charities, or any other group that has a standing in your community. You can participate in fund-raising campaigns, radio and television programs, house to house canvassing, or any other way in which you can be helpful.

Generally there are important people who are affiliated with these charitable groups. One sure way to meet these people is to be engaged in similar activities. Soon, you will be known to many of these people and when you need their aid or support, it will be simple for you to appeal to them for assistance in your career.

5. When you do meet important people who might help you in your career, show a sympathetic and understanding attitude towards them and their problems. As a rule most people think of highly placed people as being isolated from human emotions in their Olympian positions. However, many such people are lonely and eager for someone to talk to.

The story is told of a man named James Adamson, who was trying to get an order for $90,000 from the big businessman, George Eastman. He was told when he entered the great man's presence not to take more than five minutes of his time and then leave immediately. When this man was admitted to Eastman's office he instantly admired the beauty of the surroundings and complimented him on his good taste in furnishing it so tastefully. Eastman then began to tell him about some wooden chairs he has just bought and repainted, and he extended an invitation to Adamson to have lunch with him at his home to see the hand-painted chairs. At that luncheon Eastman poured out his heart to Adamson on all kinds of subjects and the two men became good friends. When the $90,000 order was given, who do you think Eastman chose? Of course, it was his new friend Adamson!

6. Another way by which you will meet wealthy and prominent people is at the playgrounds they select for their vacations. It is as easy for you to choose a spot for your vacation where important people go as it is to select some out-of-the-way spot. In the winter

these wealthy people go to such places as Palm Springs, near Los Angeles; Acapulco, in Mexico, which is a favorite resort place for many prominent people; Miami Beach, Palm Beach, and Saint Petersburg, in Florida; Honolulu; cruises on the Caribbean; the Bahamas, the West Indies, and the Virgin Islands.

In the summer of course, these wealthy persons go regularly to such world capitals as London, Paris, Rome and Athens. You can often meet them on airplanes or boats and trains. If you show yourself interested in them and project friendliness, you will be invited by them to their homes when they return from vacations.

A young man and his wife were on the way to Rome. On the same plane there was a courteous gentleman who was from the oil-rich kingdom of Libya. They struck up a conversation and before they arrived in Rome they had been invited to spend several weeks with him in Paris and at his villa in Switzerland—all expenses paid! This led to a very good friendship that later paid rich dividends for the young businessman, as he was in insurance and the friendly Libyan gave him his future business when he came to America.

7. Always give that little extra measure of personal attention and service to any person who comes into your business place. You may be a secretary or switchboard operator, but if you are courteous and kind, you cannot help but attract interest.

A young lady who wanted to be a writer once worked at the Mount Sinai Hospital in New York City, in the private pavillion, where wealthy patients were often admitted. One day, she waited on the noted writer Fannie Hurst, and she was so courteous that Fannie Hurst stopped to chat with her whenever she visited her sick friend, Jascha Heifitz, the famous violinist. The girl who worked at the switchboard during the day and studied writing at night wrote a letter to Fannie Hurst, asking her advice as to her future career as a writer. The great writer sent her a most encouraging letter which so inspired the girl that she went on to become a noted writer in her own field as a great novelist.

8. When you do meet people who are important and who might help you in your career, do not come right out and ask them to help you. You can influence such a person to volunteer his help by

showing an attitude of cooperation with him. Make him want to help you by showing him you respect his judgment and admire his achievements. It flatters any person when someone admires his accomplishments and it makes him more than willing to assist such a person.

9. Avoid controversial topics of conversation with people you have just met and who might be able to help you. Any person who is important and successful has usually won the right to having his own way. He does not like opposition; make it easy to get along with you by agreeing with him in what he says. This is especially true if he asks your opinion on some special subject.

10. Ask the advice of an important person, if you want to make him feel closer to you. Start by saying, "There's something I'd like your advice about. . . ."

This shows you believe in the superior quality of his intellect and it flatters him to think you have turned to him for advice because you know his background and experience qualify him to give you such advice.

Many times an important or wealthy person will become interested in your career if you ask him which one of two courses open to you should be taken for success.

A man who was a vice president of a large corporation was asked by a young man who wanted to get into his corporation how he should go about getting started in his career. The vice president thought for a moment and then replied, "Now that you ask, I think there's a position as a salesman in our organization, and if you qualify, you can quickly be promoted to a junior executive position at a very good salary."

This young man did not ask for a job, but he strongly hinted by asking for advice, and the executive quickly offered him his help.

Make up your mind early in your career that no person ever built his future success alone. There always have been others who have gone before on the royal road to riches, and these generous souls have reached out a helping hand to those just beginning the long, upward climb on the ladder of success.

FACTS AND FALLACIES ABOUT
MONEY MAGNETISM

Fallacies	*Facts*
The only way you can get money is to work hard for it.	Many people who today enjoy luxury, comfort, and riches, never worked a day in their lives. Money simply gravitates to them, and you, too, can be such a magnet.
If you were born on "the wrong side of the tracks" you are a born "loser."	You can build a million-dollar consciousness and begin in this moment to think, talk, look, and act like a millionaire!
You need a great deal of higher education in order to accumulate riches.	There are Golden Nuggets lying just beneath the surface of your consciousness which you may bring to the surface and these can make you rich!
The rich get richer and the poor get poorer.	Only if you *believe* it! Believing this fallacy undermines your own extranormal Powers. Your brain is a money mint and can turn out any denomination of currency that is stamped on its sensitive surface.
You are all alone in a cold, cruel world and no one *wants* to help you.	You can learn how to project money magnetism in such a way that you can influence and control rich people, making them *want* to help you!

Business acumen and technical knowledge are essential for getting rich.

There is a Psychic Money Bank that you can learn to tap that will bring you everything you desire in life. These include money, jewels, houses, land, stocks, cars, and other things of value. Develop your occult and Mystic Powers!

DECIDE RIGHT NOW THAT YOU ARE ATTRACTING MONEY—AND YOU WILL!

It is simply amazing how wealthy people *believe* they are accumulating money even when there is none in sight! Their fertile and imaginative minds are on MONEY—stocks, bonds, dividends, potential windfalls, possible deals, etc. The money they want is not in their hands, but lo and behold!—their pockets are filled! Their checkbooks reveal a bank balance of never less than six figures! Their tables are spilling over with food like a cornucopeia! They are decked out in finery! They are smiling, happy, content! There is no reason why you shouldn't share in their joy and happiness.

Your *Parker Lifetime Treasury of Occult and Mystic Powers* will activate your brain in new ways, in new channels, in almost supernatural patterns—releasing additional brainpower, psychic forces, magnetic properties. Read each paragraph slowly, perhaps the second time around. Study each clue, every hint, all suggestions and advice and keys and secrets. Get rich!

WHY YOUR OCCULT AND MYSTIC POWERS WILL MAKE WEALTHY PEOPLE HELP YOU

You are learning secrets which are unknown even to rich people! Grasp the meaning of this. By following the Money Magnetism Power-instructions in this chapter, you are placing yourself at a distinct advantage over others. You are learning how to approach, relate with, impress, and control rich people around you. They will come to your aid when you absorb the powerful secrets contained in this chapter. They won't be able to stop themselves from helping you! The Power emanating from your brain will affect all they do or say

MASTER MYSTIC KEY

1. *Always think in positive terms. Affirm: "I can get rich." "I am a magnet for money." "I image the things I want out of life." "I will think in terms of big money—$1000, $10,000, $100,000!*

2. *When in the presence of wealthy persons, show neither envy nor jealousy. They can feel your "vibrations." Offer to help them, as if their problems were greater than yours. And they will help you! Like Magic!*

3. *For at least 15 minutes per day focus your inner concentration on money and the things it can buy. Use magazine ads to help you; see the things you would like to own and impress the picture of lovely, fun-giving, life-supporting things upon your awakened brain.*

4. *Each time something in a shop window attracts you, pause and mentally declare: "I now claim these riches of the universe for my own. I desire all those objects which will add comfort and pleasure to my life."*

5. *Every day give a little extra service that will mark you as a caring, interested person. Give in the spirit you wish to receive. Think good thoughts about everyone, even strangers on the street. When you see a complete stranger walking by, say, "I hope that man (or woman) gets rich very quickly." The Karmic Law of Reciprocal Return will bring you what you wish for others!*

QUESTIONS AND ANSWERS ABOUT YOUR
NEW MYSTIC MONEY POWER

Question: I am a maid in a large motel. Can I get rich even in a thankless job like this one?
Answer: As God is no respecter of persons, so your total Mind is no respecter of occupations. It does not matter in the least what job you have or what kind of work you do. Laborers, taxi drivers, secretaries, beauticians, salesmen and saleswomen, even the jobless—all have activated their latent occult and Mystic Powers and have benefited mightily from their miraculous use.

Question: Because of my lowly job, I never get to see the big boss. How can I influence him?
Answer: Obtain any object he has handled—a piece of paper, a pen, a pencil (if he has been photographed for the newspaper, obtain a clipping of his picture). In the privacy of your home, concentrate on this object as if it were he. He will be affected to the degree that this "point of contact" is affected.

Question: The wealthy women who come into the beauty salon where I work never seem to notice me. How can I influence them to help me?
Answer: Never mind whether or not you are noticed. You are to work with your mind and your spirit. Your physical presence is only secondary now. You never know whose mind you are influencing. A young woman worked in a poodle shop for months. Wealthy ladies brought their pups in constantly and hardly gave the girl any notice. One day a very rich matron brought in her expensive poodle who had more diamonds on its collar than this young woman ever had seen in all her life. She took good care of the matron's pet, concentrating on her new Powers. Less than a year later this wealthy woman died. When the will was read (her attorneys were incredulous!), she had left her estate and wealth to the young woman—not to her greedy relatives! The young woman received $150,000 in cash! Incidentally, she also got the poodle—diamonds and all!

OCCULTOMATIC POWER STIMULATOR

1. Spend at least ten minutes a day in a "quiet time," during which you will envision some pleasurable and valued item that you cannot now afford. Obtain a picture of it if you can. Sit back, relax, gaze upon it with desire, affection, and expectancy—as if by looking at it you will force it to appear in reality right before your amazed eyes!

2. At least once a week make a short list of five or six things of beauty and fun that you would like to own. Write each one five times.

3. During working hours mull over in your mind not only the riches you wish to accumulate, but also what you will do with them once you have them. It is the height of foolishness to suddenly come by a windfall of, say $10,000, and then be so enthralled and consternated as to not know what to do with it! Many people squander their wealth because of this lack of foresight. Plan ahead!

When you once involve the thought of riches in your subconscious mind it begins to evolve the methods for you to achieve the fortune you desire.

SOME OCCULT AND MYSTIC AFFIRMATIONS
TO HELP YOU

Don't be afraid to think with Power! Affirm mentally: "I am affecting wealthy people and attracting their aid and support wherever I go."

Perish the thought that you can't get rich! Affirm: "I *am* rich! Money will follow this truth!"

Don't compare your condition with that of others—they might

not be as fortunate as they look! Affirm: "I am a unique individual and the wealth which is mine alone will come to me!"

Affirm:

Without a rich heart wealth is an ugly beggar.

> Emerson

Surplus wealth is a sacred trust which its possessor is bound to administer in his lifetime for the good of the community.

> Andrew Carnegie

Life is short. The sooner that a man begins to enjoy his wealth the better.

> Samuel Johnson

You can banish money worries forever and enjoy the security of ready cash and hefty bank accounts by using the remarkable money-magnet method.

> Norvell

POWER-POINTERS

Never doubt that money can be yours!

Belief in lack brings lack; belief in plenty brings plenty!

The quickest and easiest way to attract money is to influence wealthy people around you.

Study Norvell's "10 Ways to Meet Wealthy and Prominent People."

Most of your life you have been victimized by popular fallacies concerning Money Magnetism. Get the *facts* in this chapter of your Treasury.

Your *Parker Lifetime Treasury of Occult and Mystic Powers* is designed to get your brain working in new ways. Keep yourself receptive to powerful intuitions!

You are learning secrets which are unknown even to rich people! Use your new Power wisely!

Write out on separate paper, the five points of your Master Mystic Key. Absorb their meaning, digest their import, assimilate their Power!

It matters not at all what position you hold in physical life. Of primary importance is your control of occult and mystic forces so that they will come into play in your life to make you rich, happy, content, delighted!

Form images of the things you want, desire or need—but don't forget to image what you will do with these prizes!

Practice the Money Magnetism affirmations. Make them a part of your daily consciousness . . . And let your paranormal Powers do the rest!

Editor's Note on Power #3

This Power puts you in a position to influence people subliminally, invisibly, without their ever realizing what you are doing. Herein lies its most powerful application. Wherever you are, whatever you are doing, practice "addressing" (inwardly) the subconscious mind of others. The vibrations of your mental exercise will be transmitted energically to whomever you wish to influence.

There is no reason why you should not use the Power of Money Magnetism to better your condition and fatten your bank account. Don't permit defeatists and skeptics to discourage you. Keep your Powers secret! And go forward using them! You *deserve* more out of life and you will get it! Remember this: There is a Higher Force guiding all human activities and It ultimately decides exactly how much money each person should have. This is why some people who ask for a million dollars get only $10,000, while another person may wish for $1,000 and miraculously receive a windfall of tens of thousands! You just never know! It is best to practice your Money Magnet Power with images of vast sums of money and leave the rest to Providence.

The next Power in your growing Treasury reveals the Secret of Metaphysical Healing. If you are going to be fabulously rich, you ought to be in the peak of good health in order to enjoy your wealth to the fullest. If you suffer any ill health or if you know someone else who does, this Power will help you to cure, restore, renew, and HEAL!

POWER 4

the MIRACLE POWER OF metaphysical healing

*Colorful Secrets That Will Bring You
the Miracle of Metaphysical Healing*

h undreds of the men and women who ask Evelyn M. Monahan about metaphysical healing are worried about one thing: their health.

Some are concerned because ill health endangers their very lives. Others are troubled because afflictions bar them from "the good things in life." Still others simply desire more vitality, greater zest for living a fuller, richer life.

The various and sundry worries amount to one single concern—Health. These people certainly consulted the right person, for Evelyn Monahan as documented in her book, *Miracle of Metaphysical Healing*, knows the power of metaphysical healing from first-hand experience. "At the age of 22 years," she says, "I was faced with the prospect of living the rest of my life in a world of darkness. The head injury which had claimed my eyesight also left me with epilepsy. I experienced as many as 12 epileptic seizures a day."

And yet, this fascinating woman overcame every handicap— miraculously! Here she shares with you the power of metaphysical healing which cured her. In easy-to-read, easy-to-understand language, Miss Monahan reveals the secret power of Color-healing and she says with confidence: "Metaphysical healing is the strongest force in the entire universe, and you can begin to use this force within the next 15 minutes."

THE SECRET POWER OF
COLOR-HEALING REVEALED

Have you ever wished you lived a more colorful life? Which of us would not have our feelings hurt if we heard someone describe our personality as "colorless"? Whether or not you have realized it before, color has always played an important part in your life.

Color has a special place in your life as it has in the life of every human being on our planet. Just as important is the fact that every color is unique in itself in the properties it possesses and the effects it has on human beings. Color can not only turn people off, it can turn them on, and turning you on to good health through the use of color in the miracle of metaphysical healing is the purpose of this chapter. With the information and techniques presented to you here, you will be able to use the miracle of metaphysical healing in order to color yourself the picture of health.

SOME COLORFUL FACTS YOU SHOULD KNOW

The science of psychology has long recognized the importance of color:

Advertising companies use color psychology to make their products more pleasing to your eyes.

Color has something special to offer you on your road to perfect health.

Each color has its own vibratory pattern and its own special energy to offer you.

Through the use of your energized mind you can surround yourself with the energies of color.

Aided by your high self you can also select clothing of the colors which will be of greatest benefit to you in the area of metaphysical healing.

It is your knowledge of the universal blueprints of colors which you will gain in this chapter that will allow you to use these special properties in bringing into your life or the life of a loved one the miracle of metaphysical healing.

THE ROLE OF COLOR IN THE MIRACLE
OF METAPHYSICAL HEALING

You will be able to use a rainbow of colors which will lead you to a more precious treasure than the proverbial pot of gold. The secret properties of color presented to you here will touch your life in such a way that it can never be the same.

Study the following secrets carefully (impress them upon your mind) and know that they will be used by you to bring the glow of health to all you love.

MASTER MYSTIC KEY

The Universal Blueprints of Color and When to Use Them

1. *The universal blueprint of redness which is present in all things colored red contains the secret of unlimited energy. It contains a special energy which brings the miracle of metaphysical healing in all cases of blood disease.*

2. *The universal blueprint of blueness in all things colored blue contains unlimited energy for bringing tranquility and peace. It also possesses unlimited energies for the destruction of all forms of infection.*

3. *The universal blueprint of greenness present in all things colored green contains unlimited energy for revitalizing the nervous system, the heart, and circulatory system.*

4. *The universal blueprint for orangeness present in all things colored orange contains unlimited energy for digestion and assimilation. This special energy also includes the assimilation of oxygen through the respiratory system. It is particularly useful in the treatment of asthma and all diseases involving the lungs and chest area.*

5. *The universal blueprint of yellowness present in all things colored yellow contains unlimited energy for purification. It is especially beneficial in bringing the miracle of metaphysical healing from diseases such as diabetes and those affecting the intestines and bowels.*

6. *The universal blueprint of indigoness is present in all things colored indigo and contains unlimited energy for the treatment of all illnesses and diseases affecting the area of the head, the eyes, the ears, and the nose. It also bears unlimited energy for the treatment of mental and emotional disorders.*

7. *The universal blueprint of violetness is present in all things colored violet and contains unlimited energy for regeneration of the nervous system. The energy associated with violetness is particularly effective in curing insomnia, mental disorders resulting from brain damage, physical illness and injury affecting the brain itself, and diseases and injuries to the eyes.*

8. *The universal blueprint of whiteness is present in all things colored white and contains unlimited energy for the treatment of all disease and all injury. The miraculous energy associated with this color heals the body and mind as a whole and is especially useful when a specific diagnosis of the individual's sickness or injury has not or cannot be made.*

Now the miraculous secrets of the healing power of color are yours. From this day on you will be aware of the tremendous importance of color in your everyday life. Your mind and body are constantly absorbing the energies contained in the colors surrounding you, and with the use of your energized mind you can surround yourself with the essence of color at will.

YOUR 8-DAY RECORD OF COLOR POWER

Begin now to make a record of the above vital information so that when you, a loved one or an acquaintance needs quick help you will automatically know the appropriate color.

1st Day: Blood—think RED.
2nd Day: Infection—think BLUE.
3rd Day: Nerves, heart, circulatory system—think GREEN.
4th Day: Asthma, bronchitis, lung and chest ailments—think ORANGE.
5th Day: Diabetes, intestines and bowels troubles—think YELLOW.
6th Day: Emotional disorders—think INDIGO.
7th Day: Insomnia, mental disorders, brain injury, eye trouble—think VIOLET.
8th Day: Unspecified illness or injury—think WHITE.

Study your 8-day record daily for about a week in order to quickly associate color and sickness in one thought. You never know when you will need this information or when you will meet someone you can help instantaneously in a time of need. Say, for instance, you meet a person who complains of eyestrain. You will immediately be able to advise the use of the color violet. Learn these color-affliction correspondences! They can be a lifesaver!

HOW A MOTHER CURED HER LITTLE BOY'S ASTHMATIC ATTACKS

Janet L.'s young son was six years old when she first sought Evelyn Monahan's help. Scotty was an attractive child with an unusually appealing smile, but asthma had added a great deal of suffering to this child's life since he was three years old.

Scotty's attacks had grown more frequent and more severe since his fifth birthday; sometimes he suffered as many as three attacks a day. The best doctors and the finest medicines didn't seem to help the boy. The attacks continued.

"My son has suffered enough," Janet said. "I'm willing to do anything that will heal him and allow him to lead a normal life."

Miss Monahan gave Janet several sheets of paper explaining the universal blueprints of colors and the particular energies which each offers in the area of metaphysical healing. Janet *acted* upon the new knowledge—the same knowledge you now possess—and she applied the information about the color orange to her son.

After only one week Scotty had gone six days without an attack! After two weeks, Janet took Scotty for his checkup with the doctor. The physician's face registered his amazement that Scotty was cured! "I wish you could have been here to see the doctor's face," Janet wrote Miss Monahan. "He's taking Scotty off his medication. It's been three weeks since Scotty has had an asthmatic attack and I know that that was the last one he will ever have."

The miraculous color techniques of metaphysical healing have opened up a whole new world of alternatives to Scotty. Those same miracle techniques are now available to you—here and now!

THE 8-STEP MIRACLE TECHNIQUE
THAT COLORS ILL-HEALTH
RIGHT OUT OF YOUR LIFE

Repeat this miraculous technique three times a day. If you are using this miracle technique to restore a loved one to perfect health, insert your loved one's name in place of your own.

1. *Select a location where you are not likely to be interrupted. Lie down or sit in a chair whose back is high enough to support your head.*

2. *Close your eyes and for a moment watch your intake and outflow of breath without attempting to control the process.*

3. *Flood the screen of your mind's eye with a brilliant color*

(choose the color appropriate to the illness). With your eyes closed visualize everything around you colored a beautiful shade of this color.

4. *Through the power of your energized mind, repeat the following words to yourself mentally: "Through the miraculous force of my energized mind and the supreme intelligence of my high self, I will that the universal blueprint of ———— (insert color name here) bearing all the unlimited strength which it contains be focused immediately throughout my (or name of patient) system."*

5. *Take a deep breath through your nose and visualize the inflow of ———— (insert name of color) into your body and mind. Allow the universal blueprint to concentrate its presence and strength throughout your system and watch this occurring by creating a mental motion picture of its progress.*

6. *Allow your mind to be totally aware of the complete relaxation which flows through your body, calming and dispelling its tensions and flowing into your mind with the same peace and tranquility.*

7. *Repeat the following words to yourself mentally: "Through the miraculous power of energized mind and the unlimited energies released throughout my body by the universal blueprint of color, I am free of all sickness."*

8. *Open your eyes and go about your daily life.*

QUESTIONS AND ANSWERS ABOUT COLOR-HEALING

Question: Are all colors equally good for metaphysical healing?
Answer: It is a fact that all colors are neither good nor bad, but simply possess and radiate certain energies. However, there are times when certain colors should *not* be used. Red, for example, should not be used on a person who is emotionally upset, hysterical

or overtired. If you are emotionally distressed, avoid the color gray. And if your energy level is low, do not employ the color blue.

Question: Can the energies of colors be used for things other than illnesses?

Answer: Definitely. The calming influence of green, for instance, works miracles around people who have just suffered a tragedy or calamity. You can be of immense help to such people if you simply wear a green shirt or dress.

YOUR NEW POWER IS UNLIMITED—USE IT GENEROUSLY ON YOURSELF AND OTHERS

You have the Power to use the miracle of metaphysical healing and the miraculous color techniques presented to you here to bring peace to the most chaotic situation. You will not need tranquilizers or any drug in order to bring about this peace; you will need only the knowledge you gain in this chapter that will allow you to use the miraculous color techniques to soothe your own mind and heart and those of your loved ones.

OCCULTOMATIC POWER STIMULATOR

Your Miracle Color Technique for Becoming a Human Dynamo

Perform this miraculous technique three times a day until you notice the drastic change which will take place in your energy level. When your energy level has increased to your satisfaction, perform this miracle exercise once a day in order to maintain contact with your infinite energy source.

1. *Select a location in which you are not likely to be interrupted. Lie down or sit in a chair whose back is high enough to support your head.*

2. *Close your eyes and for a moment let your consciousness be aware of your own intake and outflow of breath without any attempt to control the process.*

3. *Allow your consciousness to be flooded with the color red. The universal blueprint for redness will radiate its infinite energy throughout your awareness.*

   With the eye of your inner mind follow the universal blueprint of redness as it fills your mind and your body.

4. *Take a deep breath through your nostrils and visualize yourself inhaling redness itself. Relax your stomach muscles immediately and allow your consciousness to follow the color red as it fills every ·area of your body and mind. Repeat this process three times and with each intake of breath be aware of the increased energy which is made available to you.*

5. *Repeat the following words to yourself mentally: "Through the use of my energized mind I am able to take full advantage of the limitless energy which the universal blueprint of redness makes available to me. My mind and body are flooded with infinite energy and all tiredness and fatigue have left me and been replaced with an inexhaustible supply of pure energy. My high self, through the power of my energized mind, will keep me in constant touch with my own source of infinite power."*

6. *Again take a deep breath, extending the diaphragm, and visualize yourself inhaling the universal blueprint of redness. Relax your stomach muscles completely and allow your consciousness to follow the path of redness throughout your entire mind and body as it makes available to each of your cells an infinite amount of energy. Repeat this process three times, and with each repetition allow yourself to be more aware of the inexhaustible source of power made available to you.*

7. *Allow your consciousness to be totally aware of your own breathing process. Make no attempt to control the intake and outflow of breath, but only watch your breathing through the eyes of your consciousness*

> *Allow yourself to be aware of the new energy which flows through you and the infinite source of energy which stands ready to serve you at will.*

8. *Open your eyes and go about your daily life.*

POWER-POINTERS

Color has a special place in your life as an aid to metaphysical healing.

Each color has its own vibratory pattern and its own special energy to offer you.

The Universal Blueprints of Color are:

1. RED—blood diseases.
2. BLUE—infections.
3. GREEN—nerves, heart, and circulatory troubles.
4. ORANGE—Asthma, bronchitis, lung ailments.
5. YELLOW—Diabetes, intestines and bowel ills.
6. INDIGO—Emotional disorders.
7. VIOLET—Insomnia, mental illness, eye trouble.
8. WHITE—Unspecified ailments.

Remember that a caring mother cured her only son of terrible asthmatic attacks through metaphysical healing with color. And the boy was only six years old!

Study and *practice* the 8-Day Miracle Technique. Remember above all: Your new Power is unlimited!

Editor's Note on Power #4

Re-examine carefully the 8-Step Miracle Technique, for this is Miss Monahan's greatest contribution to your new knowledge of metaphysical healing. Follow each instruction to the letter. Practice the exercise dutifully.

Observe men and women who are in need of some metaphysical aid and do your best to assist them. You can do this unobtrusively by wearing colors you know will be conducive to their good health. And your own health will improve too!

Make a written record of any case history, Question and Answer, or Master Mystic Key and Occultomatic Power Stimulator that "rings a bell" with you. You might develop the self-help habit of underscoring pertinent passages throughout this Treasury with colored pencils. This will facilitate easy reference later when you re-study the amazing facts about occult and mystic Powers.

> The next Power in your growing Treasury is MAGIC! It provides you with the key to using actual magical processes for increasing your success rate, developing greater personal Power, and enjoying more out of life.

Before proceeding, however, it is time to pause for a little test which will help you to progress faster.

YOUR PARKER PROSPERITY PROGRESS REPORT #1

The following brief quiz will:

1. Reinforce your absorption of the first third of your Parker Lifetime Treasury of Occult and Mystic Powers.
2. Establish an intimate and life-long connection between your mind and the Powers at your disposal.

Instructions:

Each of the following questions is to be answered *True* or *False*. Take this little test using a separate sheet of paper. *Important*: Do not write directly in the book as this will distort or negate the results. It will help you to recall important keys and clues while at the same time help you to recognize weak spots in your progress.

At the end of the test are instructions for scoring your results. This score will tell you how you are doing as a new Power-holder, revealing the degree of your progress—which will accelerate steadily as you proceed along the road to Prosperity with the aid of your Parker Powers.

Get comfortable. Relax. Take this test.

1. My life is predestined and there isn't much I can do to change it.
2. One-tenth of my brainpower is all I can expect to be able to use.
3. Rest is essential for unleashing one's occult and mystic powers.
4. When you work with your brain you need more sleep and rest than when you work with muscle alone.
5. There is no way to get rid of worries.
6. The Miracle Mind Magic Stimulator works only if you already possess psychic ability.
7. Visualizing a dream, goal or wish is an important aspect of the Miracle Mind Magic Stimulator.
8. One should practice intensifying the Miracle Mind Magic Stimulator about once a year.
9. It is not right for a person to desire riches.
10. The Miracle Mind Magic Stimulator is good for obtaining a marriage partner, but not for winning contests.
11. Luck is haphazard and you just have to wait for it to change for the better.
12. Note-taking helps to impress the subconscious mind with the tips and keys you are receiving from this book's occult and mystic Masters.
13. The careful study of Power #1 prepares you for Power #2.
14. The Fiery Serpent is a mythical snake.
15. Bill and Emmy D. tried the occult and mystic way to success and failed miserably.
16. Progress is not as important in psychic de-

velopment as it is in practical, scientific fields.

17. Anyone can cultivate a "sixth sense."
18. The Sixth Sense is something you achieve after death.
19. You don't have to worry about the way you breathe so long as you concentrate well.
20. *"Prana"* means "psychic breath."
21. Psychic breathing and mental imagery work together to create miracles.
22. The seven Vital Centers of the body are known as "Chakras."
23. Writing our wishes, dreams and goals helps manifest them in reality.
24. "Kundalini" is the Sanskrit term for an energy field which resides in each of us.
25. The magical word OM summons Kundalini.
26. It's quite all right to use your occult and mystic Powers against others so long as you come out ahead.
27. One of the greatest achievements gained by the advanced student of the occult is his ability to create by the power of thought.
28. You don't have to *believe* in success if you know the secret technique for achieving it.
29. If you are going to get rich yourself, the best thing to do is to avoid other rich people.
30. Knowing the Mystic Secret to Money Power can pyramid your wealth.
31. It is best to ask for help from every rich and influential person you encounter.
32. The only way you can get money is to work hard for it.
33. If you were born on "the wrong side of the tracks" you are a born "loser."
34. There are Golden Nuggets lying just beneath

the surface of your consciousness which you
may bring to the surface and these can make
you rich.
35. Your brain is a money mint.
36. No one wants to help you in this world.
37. Business acumen and technical knowledge
are essential for getting rich.
38. If you decide right now that you are attracting money like a magnet, you will.
39. With the proper development of your occult
and mystic Powers you can *make* wealthy
people help you.
40. It makes no difference what job you hold or
what kind of work you do, occult and mystic
Powers can increase your wealth.
41. Only doctors and medicine cure sick people.
42. Color has no healing qualities, but it is pleasant to have in a sickroom.
43. Turning you on to good health through the
use of color is metaphysical healing.
44. Each color has its own vibratory pattern and
its own special energy to offer you.
45. Knowledge of the Universal Blueprints of
Color can bring me the glow of health.
46. If someone I know has a blood disease I
should think of the color Blue.
47. You can cure asthma with color, but nasal
sprays are quicker.
48. The 8-Day Miracle Technique colors ill-
health right out of your life.
49. There is no miraculous technique to practice
in order to increase one's energy.
50. A good self-habit to cultivate is to create a
Personal Power Notebook in which to copy
down, word for word, pertinent passages that
have special meaning to you.

How To Record Your Progress

The following statements should have been marked *True*: 3, 4, 7, 12, 13, 17, 20, 21, 22, 23, 24, 25, 27, 30, 34, 35, 38, 39, 40, 43, 44, 45, 48, 50.

All others—*False*.

Each entry is worth 2 points. For each right answer add two points to get your total score. A score of 50 to 60 is FAIR; 60 to 70, SATISFACTORY; 70 to 80, GOOD; 80 to 90, EXCELLENT; 90 to 100, EXCEPTIONAL!

Once you have added up your score (for example, 25 correct answers scores as 50—25 × 2 equals 50), return to the text and find the correct answers to your wrong entries. Do this to get straight in your mind the proper information before you go on to the second third of your accumulating Powers.

When every entry is then right, so that your score is now 100, proceed to more exciting and life-enriching occult and mystic Powers.

A Note of Caution

It is only fair to warn the reader about the psychospiritual aspects of writing in books. You will notice that the above test (and many other places in this book) provides spaces for you in which to score your answers, notes, thoughts, and insights. By all means avail yourself of this important feature—*but*—MARK THE ANSWERS IN YOUR PERSONAL POWER NOTEBOOK *ONLY*—DO NOT WRITE IN THIS BOOK UNDER ANY CIRCUMSTANCES FOR TO DO SO WILL DESTROY POTENT PSYCHIC VIBRATIONS.

There are two reasons for this precaution and they are related: One, when you respond to this book's questions, a metaphysical law requires that you transfer your reactions to a personal journal *that is totally imbued with your indelibly unique stamp*. Therefore, do not write in this book if you have borrowed it from another person, because (reason number two) writing in a book not your own *negates the Powers*. This interaction between you, your Personal Power Notebook and these pages will greatly increase the potency of the occult and mystic Powers at your disposal.

Remember, too, to pass on this metaphysical information to others if you lend your book—impress upon the borrower that he or she *must not write in a book not their own*. Better still, lend it to no one. Purchase it, own it, possess it, and treat it like a personal journal containing secrets to health, wealth and happiness!

how to increase your success rate with the power of magic

10 Fast-Working Runic Spells to Magically Smooth Your Path Through Life

You *can* use magic spells to change your luck, increase your wealth, and generally enrich your entire life.

When you really *want* (desire intensely) to increase your success rate, you will not balk at using occult and mystic incantations to work miracles in your life. You will possess this priceless Power through the practical techniques of Runic Spells—the magical method that lifts YOU out of the swamp of lack, deprivation, and poverty—even when your success doesn't seem logically possible!

Start right now by assimilating the truth about Runic Spells which mystic Frater Malak, in his book *The Mystic Grimoire of Mighty Spells and Rituals*, has revealed to thousands of aspirants throughout the nation. This basic truth is the concrete foundation of Frater Malak's whole program, the Power of which you will gain from this chapter.

HOW TO COME OUT AHEAD WITH THE MODERN USE OF MAGIC

Here is the magical truth.

Remember at all times that scientific logic forms little part of the Miracles of Magic—in fact, Magic is beyond logic as science knows it, which is exactly why the actions, words, and thoughts we use produce results which *seem*—to the scientific observer—to bear little relation to the method.

But once you have performed a Spell or Ritual and seen the miraculous results, you will be above any criticism. You will *know* that a certain Spell or Ritual produces a certain result: you will have seen it happen to you, and no amount of scientific debunking from others who have yet to understand can affect your knowledge or belief.

"You can be All Powerful," says Frater Malak. "The Universe is yours to command. What do you want? In the pages of this chapter you will find out how to get it by Magical means. Read and wonder—but suspend your disbelief in these Miracles until they have worked for you. For that is all I ask: perform these Spells and Rituals, and you will be happy, rich, and victorious."

Malak's powerful, magical instructions allow you to achieve your desires without fuss and great preparation. All you need is your desire and your energized Mind. Until you become proficient in the use of your Power of Magic, a Spell may require you to repeat it for practice before the results delight you. But you need no apparatus or profound knowledge of occult and mystic esoterica. The potent secrets are right here for your immediate use. Just carry out the simple instructions as given, and you will see your most secret wishes come true with startling and joyful ease.

This is your own private and secret Treasury of Occult and Mystic Powers. Treat it as such and completely ignore skeptics and doubters. As Malak rightly says, "The proof of Magic is in the glorious personal results!"

Are you ready? Then fasten your psychic seat belts, for you are about to receive the Power of Magic!

THE VITAL BRING-ME-WEALTH SPELL

Here is one of the easiest—yet fastest working!—Spells from Malak's repertoire. It is designed to bring you certain amounts of money—instantly and miraculously!

In absolute secrecy (other minds can interfere with your Cosmic connection) write down on a piece of paper *exactly* what you need in the way of ready cash. Keep it simple, something like this: "I need $200 for this month's rent," or "I need $24.75 to pay the electric bill." *Be specific*.

Draw a circle around your statement and keep the paper in your pocket or purse for at least 10 hours. Read it every now and then throughout the course of the day—*when you are alone and unobserved*.

In the evening, after sunset, sit alone and light a single candle. If you wish you can burn a stick of incense and have music playing (not a talk show or TV). By the light of the candle re-read your desire.

Then say:

> Beyond this light the Powers come
> To bring me this needed sum,
> Aided by a Cosmic Name
> Because I burn this Magic flame.

Repeat this Ritual three times, then extinguish the candle. Tear your paper into tiny pieces and throw them away (no other eyes must ever see them). Perform this Ritual for seven successive evenings or until the money appears, whichever occurs first.

THE TERRIFIC WIN-IT-ALL SPELL

People who have never gambled before in their lives have made big "killings" by following Malak's easy instructions. You can do the same! Learn and practice the Win-It-All Spell.

This Spell needs a private place to set the luck vibrations going your way before you join a game or place a bet. It is designed to turn luck vibrations your way.

1. Make sure you are alone and unobserved.

2. Throw your hands and arms upward and outward, move your feet about 24 inches apart, so that you are standing in the shape of an X.

3. If it is daytime, perform this easy Ritual facing the sun. If it is after dark, face west if you are performing the Ritual before midnight, east if after midnight.

4. Intone (or mentalize if you may be overheard):

> Sun! Sun! The powers that be,
> The Gods of Chance shall smile on me,
> While Lady Luck shall steal away
> The fortune from my rivals' play.

HOW ALICE L. LEFT A LIFE OF POVERTY AND BECAME A RICH GAMBLER AFTER WORKING THE TERRIFIC WIN-IT-ALL SPELL

Faro is Alice L.'s game, and she's rich—but if you'd told her a while ago that she would be in that situation, she'd have laughed in your face.

Sickness and pain had been Alice's lot for years, and the climax of misery came when her doctor told her she must have expensive liver surgery or resign herself to a short life of agony and woe.

"Lack of the necessary cash was only part of it," she said. "My husband was also ailing with a lung problem, and our four children were none too healthy.

"We did our best to keep things half decent, but debts were accumulating, and my bad news seemed to be the final blow which would send us all to the poorhouse."

Alice was at her wit's end. Only a massive injection of cash into their household would save them. She bought lottery tickets. No luck. She entered competitions. Nothing. Appeals to relatives found them uncooperative. Meanwhile, Alice's pains became worse.

"I could hardly move, and I was constantly exhausted, and the house was a mess," she recalled. "I hadn't the will to lift a finger most of the time.

"Then one day, as I was in a half-awake state of agony and insomnia, I had this dream. It was weird: I was working a Spell."

Alice doesn't know to this day where the dream came from. Her maternal grandmother was psychic and used to read a great many mystic books, so Alice supposes she may have read the Spell when she was younger and then forgotten about it.

"I came back to full consciousness, but the dream was still with me. I recalled it all clearly, and I took it as a sign," she said. "A friend had recently given me a booklet of coupons from Mr. Sy's casino in Vegas. We lived only a short distance from the city, so I left a note for my husband and kids and took a bus. I thought I must be out of my mind, but some inner force urged me on."

Alice used the booklet to collect $36 in nickels and tokens at the casino, and she then retired to the washroom.

"I whispered the words of the Spell and started the most fantastic day of my life," she said. "Almost every time I laid down a chip at a game, I won. After dark, I called my husband. He was frantic—thought I'd gone around the bend. I jingled a pile of silver dollars at him over the phone and told him to come and meet me."

The sparkling stream of luck held for Alice—and has held steady to this day. Within a week, she had enough winnings to move the family into Vegas.

"I still think I'm dreaming," she said. "To think that a few words could work a miracle like the one we're living.

"The casinos welcome me in. Don't you believe those stories about big winners being asked to stay away: the casinos are always pleased to see me, because I invariably collect a big crowd of people—who are maybe not as lucky as me."

Alice had her operation, and it was a total success. She paid for it easily from her newfound wealth. She has now furnished an opulent home in the most exclusive part of the city. Her husband drives her to the casinos in a limousine rigged with every imaginable electronic gadget, including TV and a bar. Their parties and gifts to charity are the talk of the town.

"We're a healthy, ecstatic family now," Alice said. "What a contrast from a few months back. We've invested our cash and live high-on-the-hog off the interest.

"But I still try the Terrific Win-It-All Spell occasionally, just to have the joy of seeing Magic in action again."

PRACTICE MAKES PERFECT IN MAGIC, TOO!

Practice these two Spells repeatedly, every chance you get, before going on to Malak's more complicated and potent Rituals. Get the "Magic habit." Set up those vibrations which are so essential to successful results in Magic.

Remember: Practice makes perfect!

THE AMAZING ROULETTE-CERTAINTY SPELL

This particular Spell may be used wherever you need a Lucky Number. Malak shows you step-by-step how to develop your personal number of magical Power:

1. Write down your birth date in figures. If, for example, you were born on August 10, 1934, you would write: 8/10/1934.

2. Add these numbers together, for example: 8 plus 1 plus 0 plus 1 plus 9 plus 3 plus 4—which comes to 26.

3. Whatever result you get, always keep adding figures until you reduce it to one single digit. In the above example: 2 plus 6 equals 8.

4. This single digit is your Destiny Number.

HOW TO FIND YOUR LUCKY NAME NUMBER

Now print your name (as you sign it on a check) on a piece of paper. Give each letter of your name the value indicated in this chart:

1	2	3	4	5	6	7	8	9
A	B	C	D	E	F	G	H	I
J	K	L	M	N	O	P	Q	R
S	T	U	V	W	X	Y	Z	

Example: Let's say a woman named Jane Smith was born on August 10, 1934. She already has her Destiny Number. Now, on the piece of paper on which she has printed her name, she adds the corresponding figures, like this:

J A N E   S M I T H
1 1 5 5   1 4 9 2 8

Do the same thing with your name! Then add up the figures. Jane Smith's would be developed in this way:

First total: 36

Second total: (3 plus 6) equals 9.

Jane Smith's Lucky Number is 9.

Now Jane Smith (and you!) have two numbers so far: Jane's being 8 (Destiny Number) and 9 (Lucky Name Number). One more figure is needed—the number of the hour in which you intend to get rich.

MALAK'S TABLE OF REIGNING NUMBERS OF EACH HOUR OF THE DAY

By consulting the following chart you can obtain the third number you need:

TIME	NUMBER OF THE HOUR
Midnight to 12.59 a.m.	1
1.00 a.m. to 1.59 a.m.	2
2.00 a.m. to 2.59 a.m.	3
3.00 a.m. to 3.59 a.m.	4
4.00 a.m. to 4.59 a.m.	5
5.00 a.m. to 5.59 a.m.	6
6.00 a.m. to 6.59 a.m.	7
7.00 a.m. to 7.59 a.m.	8
8.00 a.m. to 8.59 a.m.	9
9.00 a.m. to 9.59 a.m.	1
10.00 a.m. to 10.59 a.m.	2

11.00 a.m. to 11.59 a.m.	**3**
Noon to 12.59 p.m.	**4**
1.00 p.m. to 1.59 p.m.	**5**
2.00 p.m. to 2.59 p.m.	**6**
3.00 p.m. to 3.59 p.m.	**7**
4.00 p.m. to 4.59 p.m.	**8**
5.00 p.m. to 5.59 p.m.	**9**
6.00 p.m. to 6.59 p.m.	**1**
7.00 p.m. to 7.59 p.m.	**2**
8.00 p.m. to 8.59 p.m.	**3**
9.00 p.m. to 9.59 p.m.	**4**
10.00 p.m. to 10.59 p.m.	**5**
11.00 p.m. to 11.59 p.m.	**6**

YOUR LUCKY NUMBER: HOW TO FIND IT
AND HOW TO USE IT

1. Obtain your "Destiny Number" by totaling the figures of your Birth Date as per the above instructions.

2. Obtain your "Lucky Name Number" by totaling the figures of your Name as per the above instructions.

3. Obtain the "Number of the Hour" from the above chart.

4. Now add these three numbers together, reducing all totals to a single digit. Using our example of Jane Smith, who has decided to try her luck at 10.00 a.m., we discover her LUCKY NUMBER like this:

a. Her Destiny Number is 8.

b. Her Name Number is 9.

c. Her Hour Number is (according to the chart) 2.

d. Therefore her LUCKY NUMBER is the total of these three: 8 plus 9 plus 2 or 19. To reduce the last number to a single digit, add the figures together: 1 plus 9 is 10. It's still a double digit. Add them *again*. 1 plus 0 equals 1. The LUCKY NUMBER of Jane Smith is 1.

Do the same with your *own* numbers!

HOW TO CHANGE YOUR LUCK FOR THE
BETTER WITH YOUR LUCKY NUMBER

Once you have your LUCKY NUMBER, you are ready to put it to work. Let's say, for example, you are interested in roulette. Find yourself a place at a roulette table, have a few chips ready, and then check the time. Add together your NAME NUMBER, your DESTINY NUMBER, and the HOUR NUMBER (as done above). The final single digit is your Bet Number.

As soon as you've discovered your Bet Number, pay attention to the croupier. Sit back and watch the roll of the little ball. The spins of the wheel you're going to bet on are the ones which correspond to your Bet Number. Frater Malak has developed a handy Table of Corresponding Numbers for you, so you need figure no further. Here are your Bet Numbers (whether you are playing roulette, betting on a horse, entering a contest, or whatever):

YOUR LUCKY NAME NUMBER	CORRESPONDING ROULETTE WHEEL NUMBERS TO BET ON
1	1, 10, 19, 28
2	2, 11, 20, 29
3	3, 12, 21, 30
4	4, 13, 22, 31
5	5, 14, 23, 32
6	6, 15, 25, 33
7	7, 16, 25, 34
8	8, 17, 26, 35
9	9, 18, 27, 36

MASTER MYSTIC KEY

The Powers governing personal gambling luck are easily influenced, but notoriously fickle for that same reason.

It is possible for others involved in a game with you to be—deliberately or unknowingly—using a Spell or Ritual which at that time is more powerful than yours (for Cosmic reasons). This will naturally affect, and possibly cancel, your own Magic. In that case—and you will recognize this by the fact that your early bets are losers—leave the arena at once and return at some other, more favorable, time.

SOME OTHER SPELLS AND RITUALS TO ENHANCE EVERY ASPECT OF YOUR LIFE

Spells and Rituals may be used successfully in other areas of your life. They are presented here now for your edification and gratification, for your Parker Treasury is designed to enhance all spheres of your life.

The Tantalizing New-Strength Spell

Before you retire for the night, place a piece of string about six inches long under your pillow. As you relax in bed, lie on your back, slip your right hand beneath the pillow and touch the string. Say aloud (or mentally):

> Powers of Sun and Moon and Light
> Come to me in the still of night.

Pull the string from under your pillow, and hold it in front of your chest as you tie a single knot in it. Say aloud (or in your head):

> This knot shall raise me to a peak
> Almighty strong—no longer weak.

Replace the string under your pillow, turn over, and go to sleep. Repeat this Ritual on the following two nights (three times in all). Then place the knotted string (it now has three knots!) in your pocket or purse and carry it about with you for 28 days. "This Spell," says occultist Malak, "works best if you start it on the night of the New Moon."

THREE VIGOROUS SPELLS TO RESTORE
YOUR HEALTH, BEAUTY AND POTENCY

Think of someone you greatly admire and consider his or her attributes which you would like to possess. Then intone this Magic Incantation:

The Tremendous Beauty-Is-Mine Spell

> Healing rays now begin
> To bring new beauty pouring in.

Whenever you are in sunlight, close your eyes for a few seconds and mentally intone this Spell. *Feel* the sun on your face. Do this for 28 days.

The Stupendous Young-Again Spell

Would you like to appear younger, lovelier, more attractive? Try this amazing Spell. Hold a photograph of yourself, taken when you were younger (if a photo of yourself is not available, use a picture of a glamorous or handsome person). Then . . .

1. Fill a glass with water and cover it with a saucer and place it on a windowsill during a sunny day.

2. At midnight (Full Moon is the best time) sit in a darkened room lit by a single candle. Set the glass of water on the table. Remove the saucer.

3. Hold the picture so you can see it by the light of the candle.

4. Say aloud or mentally (remembering that secrecy is desirable):

> Time reverse your steady flow.
> In mind and body back I go
> Far in the realms of space and plane
> I drink at the Fountain of Youth again.

5. Set the picture down to the left of the candle. Lift the glass with your right hand and drink some of the elixir.

The Exciting Brilliance-for-Me Spell

This Spell works best if it is first worked three days before the Moon is full, on a clear night when you can stand, either outside or at a window, with the moonlight shining on your face.

Gaze steadily into the silver disc of the Moon and intone:

> Luna, Luna, polished bright
> Clean my mind, my soul, my sight,
> Let a flame of brilliance grow
> All is clear. I see. I know.

OCCULTOMATIC POWER STIMULATOR

The Powers you command are the very Forces of Creation. You will be using methods which have been learned by tedious experiment and time-consuming research from the Soul of Nature Herself.

Write out the Spells and Rituals. Practice each diligently. The rewards will be great.

Be happy, be strong, and be powerful—all with the cooperation of these Cosmic Forces which will work for your good.

Memorize the Power Spells you can until they are second nature to you. Use them daily to create remarkable changes in your life.

Here are three Spells for warding off psychic attack and bullying enemies—Self-Protection Spells.

THREE SELF-PROTECTION SPELLS THAT THWART ENMITY AND ADVERSITY

When someone plagues you with negativity, say this Spell:

> The troubles and forces I send to thee
> Shall never return to trouble me.

Then, while focusing your thoughts on the person who causes you trouble, intone this Spell:

Stir in your sleep and feel the effects
Of all that I send thee in the Name of this Hex.
From fiends of your mind shall your consciousness
        cower,
Stir in thy brain as I pour in my Power.

The Unseen Inner-Plane-Travel Spell

This Spell takes you wherever you wish to go to alter the thinking of negative people. Find a place and time where you can relax. Decide where you wish to be and who you wish to influence with Power. Take six deep breaths and mentally repeat seven times:

Distance, darkness, fade away
I seek the Mystic Traveling Ray
Reveal before my mind's bright eye
The person whom I wish to espy.

The Crushing Disharmony-Exorcising Spell

This Spell is designed to produce harmony between people who are at odds with each other. It can be used to such ends as stopping married couples from quarreling or promoting mutual admiration between a boss and a worker.
Envision the people in question and intone:

In the Name above all other Names
I bring peace and harmonious aims
Replace war and strife
With cooperative life
Let the discord be burned up in flames

QUESTIONS AND ANSWERS ABOUT
SUCCESS-BUILDING MAGIC IN
TWENTIETH-CENTURY AMERICA

Question: Isn't it devilish to use Spells and Rituals?
Answer: Over the centuries a myth has grown up that in order to work Magic you must use the Devil's powers or sign a pact with

him. Let me assure you at the outset that every Cosmic Power in this book is good, benevolent, and success-building.

Question: Other people are luckier than I am. What can I do to change all that?

Answer: That's what this Treasury is all about! This book can bring you the lucky breaks you require—the whole Secret of Magic: ways of performing simple acts which produce amazing results. These are designed with your success and happiness in mind.

POWER-POINTERS

Read your Parker Treasury through. Then come back and study each power-packed chapter carefully. Make notes. Record your thoughts and insights, as well as instructions and hints and keys. And practice the techniques!

Remember: You *can* use magic Spells and Rituals to change your luck, increase your wealth, and generally enrich your entire life.

This is your own private collection of occult and mystic Powers. Treat it as such and completely ignore skeptics and doubters. It is not the opinions of others but the results you achieve that will convince you of your Powers.

Make a list of the Spells and Rituals in this chapter. Get familiar with the terminology—this also helps set up benevolent vibrations between you and Cosmic Powers.

Editor's Note on Power #5

Apply all the instructions to work your Spells and Rituals, and you have the equivalent of a well-tuned car, which will take you wherever you wish to go. If you should have to omit a few details—don't worry!—it will be like driving an older model automobile: it will still get you to your desired destination, even if not so quickly. Whenever possible, however, attend to as many details as you can—study and practice—and you will enhance your certainty of getting what you want as quickly and automatically as you wish.

The next chapter provides you with one of the most amazing Powers known—*Mana-Force*. The famed psychic authority Madeleine Morris will show you step-by-step how to summon the mightiest occult force known to man. This Power will work miracles in your life.

POWER 6

mana-force:
the power of
phenomenal good luck

*How to Command Lady Luck for Hidden
Treasure and Fabulous Fortune*

Ben and Karen T., of Topeka, Kansas, lived in a small apartment with their three small children, two girls and a boy. Ben drove to work in a local factory in a battered old car; Karen's days were occupied with caring for the little ones, doing endless laundry, and housecleaning. Life was hard, money tight, bills overwhelming. Ben and Karen had few luxuries and very little pleasure—a night out perhaps once a month to attend a movie or have a pizza.

Suddenly, within a few months, Ben was vice-president of a corporation, driving to the office in a new Cadillac; Karen had a maid to do the laundry and housecleaning, the children spent their happy days in an expensive pre-school, and her days were filled with new and exciting social and community activities.

What could have caused such a drastic and remarkable change in Ben and Karen's lives?

"Luck," says Karen with twinkling eyes and smiling lips. "Phenomenal good luck!"

It is this kind of luck which Madeleine C. Morris, ordained minister of the Church of Cosmic Wisdom in Hawaii, reveals in *Miracle of Mana Force: Secret of Wealth, Love and Power*.

"My techniques will give you fun and rewards heretofore undreamed of," promises Mrs. Morris. "You will learn that Lady Luck is truly a creature who you can bend to your will. Her power is unlimited and *you* will find out how to control her so she can serve you."

MANA-FORCE CHARMETRICS

The Power of Luck which this chapter offers you will imbue you with the magnetic force of Charmetrics, a secret process developed by Mrs. Morris, which results in treasure-building and fortune-finding miracles that will astound you. Phyllis F. used it to find some valuable antiques that brought her fantastic profits in her business. Jack J. used it to win $400 in one evening in Las Vegas. Warren G. used it to bring a small fortune to himself. Jed F. found a fortune while he was on an ordinary fishing trip.

QUESTIONS AND ANSWERS
CONCERNING YOUR POWER OVER
LUCK, CHANCE, AND TREASURE

Question: My husband is unemployed, our son can't get a job, I've been sick for months and can't help out. Can Mana-Force change a situation as bad as this?

Answer: With Lady Luck on your side, the dam will burst and all of the treasures of the world will come tumbling into your life. You have only to put in your order and she will change your life.

Question: What do you mean by Lady Luck?

Answer: Lady Luck is like a Familiar. Now, don't think in terms of a witch's cat—that is exaggerated superstition. A real Familiar is a creature created by Mind on the astral plane. Probably the most powerful Familiar known to man is Lady Luck. Yes, she is real. Her Power has been reinforced over and over again down through the ages by believing men and women. She has been worshipped by many as a Goddess. Luck is very real. Since she is a Familiar, she must be told *what* to do and when.

Question: Do you mean that I can command Luck?

Answer: Absolutely! If you don't command Luck, you do not *have* Luck. Bad luck, by the way, is simply the absence of human control and command!

Question: How can I control and command Lady Luck to smile in my life?

Answer: Let's suppose that Lady Luck is commanded to make you win at roulette. She can stop the *Astral* wheel at any number that would make you win. The roulette wheel in the room where you are gambling will stop at the same number.

Question: But that sounds so easy! Is it?

Answer: Yes, YES!—If you know the secret!

MASTER MYSTIC KEY

If you will give your command in the proper manner, Lady Luck *will* obey you. All she needs from you is direction and the Power which will motivate her. It is important to remember that she is a Familiar—a servant awaiting your explicit instructions as to what you want her to do. She will not take the initiative but she *will* obey your commands. She must do as she is ordered. She was created for this very purpose.

You will now be given the magic key for turning her on.

THE MORRIS PLAN FOR YOUR CONTROL AND COMMAND OF PHENOMENAL GOOD LUCK

Get alone with yourself, and follow these instructions carefully—and you will be amazed at the life-enriching results! Do you want instant riches? Can you use more money? How about a new car or clothes or food or just good old-fashioned fun and luxury? Make a wish, follow the steps for increasing your Luck Power, and rake in untold riches. It's as easy as A, B, C!

MAGIC LUCK MAGNET RITUAL

A. Give Instructions to Low Self

This is a very important step in the Magic Luck Magnet ritual. The success of this ritual depends upon a three-way participation.

You will use your conscious mind and will to order Lady Luck to carry out your wishes. You will instruct the low self by giving it directions to work with Lady Luck. I think I can best explain this by giving you a graphic example of how this would work in a specific instance.

Let us assume that you wish to win at roulette. You would tell your low self that this is your wish. You would tell it to contact Lady Luck and find out exactly what she was going to do to bring about your winnings. Your low self and Lady Luck can communicate quite easily because they can both operate on the astral level. The low self has the added advantage of being able to communicate directly with your conscious mind.

Now the low self has found out that Lady Luck is going to stop the wheel on #4. You will get an urge from your low self to put your chips on #4. Presto, you win. Of course, there are many different ways that these same winnings could be brought about. I have only cited this one as a way that it *could* happen.

I also used this example to show you how your low self becomes involved in the magic luck magnet ritual.

You can see how necessary it is that you obtain the participation of your low self in working with Lady Luck. So, in your instructions to your low self, tell it just that. You wish to have its cooperation in working with Lady Luck. Tell your low self that you want it to signal you of any conscious act you need to make.

Your low self is a childlike creature who likes to play games—just as any child does. So tell your low self that this is a game that you, Lady Luck, and your low self are going to play. It really is a game, after all. So you are telling the truth. Tell your low self that the reward will be a lot of money—or whatever the reward is. You will be amazed at how easy it will be to get the cooperation of your low self with this approach.

B. Build Mana-Force Field

The first step in the magic luck magnet ritual is to build a strong force field of Mana-Force Power. As you have learned in previous chapters, this will give your ritual power and impetus. It will create a powerful medium through which your command will travel to obtain the desired result.

1. Take six deep breaths, holding each one as long as you can before taking the next.
2. After the first three breaths, hold your hands out in front of you, palms facing. Feel the tingling between the palms as the force field becomes more intensified.
3. After you have built your force field, be still for a few moments and be aware of the tremendous amount of living energy you have generated.

C. Send Your Command to Lady Luck

Now you are going to use the tremendous charge of Mana-Force Power you have generated to send your command to Lady Luck. She will also be given a surge of energy from the mana you send to her. From this part of the ritual, she will receive her directions and will be given the added energy to act in your behalf.

Your command must be spoken in a firm voice with authority. The Mana-Force Power you have generated will give your command tremendous power. If you speak your command, *knowing* it will be obeyed, *it will be obeyed*. The being that you are directing your command to does not have the will to disobey a strong command. Instructions given by an authoritative human must be obeyed.

There is one more thing that you must do to have your wishes followed. You must *know* with all your heart that you will get what you ask for. Indecision will weaken any command you give. So as you give your command, and after it has been given, don't let the tiniest doubt creep into your mind. Why should you? *You* have spoken the word. All you have to do now is wait for your wish to be fulfilled.

The command that you give to Lady Luck will depend on what you want her to bring to you. Suppose you wish to win money at Las Vegas, the race track, or any other game of chance. A command like this could be given: "Lady Luck, I *command* you to bring me winnings of ($100, $500, $10,000 or whatever you can truly believe you can get—keep the amount believable to you). I command this with my full heart and soul. So be it. It is done.''

If you want to win a car, a house or find a winning answer to a quiz, give the command to Lady Luck to make this prize come to you. Once again, speak your command with authority and then *know* that the prize is on its way to you.

Remember, Lady Luck will obey a confident master. Be that master and know the joy of having Lady Luck work *with* you. You have the most powerful persuader in existence—Mana-Force Power. With this and Lady Luck on your side, you can't lose.

OCCULTOMATIC POWER STIMULATOR

It is wise to *practice* giving authoritative commands to Lady Luck to assure pleasing and gratifying wish-fulfillment.

In your Personal Power Notebook, write down half a dozen wishes you would like to see come true in your private life. Perform Part B of the Morris Plan: *Build Mana-Force Field*. Then write out the most powerful authoritative commands you can think of, at least two per wish. Write your wishes and commands, on separate pieces of paper, in two columns, just as follows:

Wish	*Command*
1.	1. ....
	....
2.	2. ....
	....
3.	3. ....
	....
4.	4. ....
	....
5.	5. ....
	....
6.	6. ....
	....

THE HIDDEN TREASURES YOUR MANA-FORCE
POWER CAN UNEARTH FOR YOU

We are all familiar with treasure chests that were buried by the pirates of old. There are countless stories telling us of old sailing ships that went down, carrying gold bullion and gems. However, these are not the treasures I am going to tell you about. Our modern day treasures abound everywhere. There are untold acres of land bearing precious metals that have never been mined. There are deposits of gems in the earth just waiting to be discovered. There are personal treasures that have been buried in back yards or hidden in the attics of old houses. Many undiscovered legacies lie hidden everywhere, from unlisted bank safety deposits to old mattresses. Then there are the countless items that might not be recognized as treasures to one person, while they may be worth more than gold to another.

But what good are all these treasures if they remain hidden? It is only when they are discovered and put to use that they become of some intrinsic value to someone. There is a way that these treasures can be sought and located. Yes, and many of them can bring a fabulous fortune to their discoverer. There is no reason in the world why you should not be such a lucky discoverer!

Make a list of treasures you would like to find. Don't think in terms of pirates' gold or sunken chests of jewelry—think of local things, like a single stamp on an old forgotten letter which is worth $200,000; old coins worth a great deal of cold hard cash to a dealer; uranium discovered on a small piece of "worthless" property.

The fantastic ritual that follows will lead you to any treasure that you seek!

HOW TO USE YOUR MANA-FORCE
POWER IN THE AMAZING
REVEAL-TREASURE-TO-ME RITUAL

A. Give Instructions to Low Self

Make it clear to the low self what it is that you wish to find. Talk to it as though you were giving instructions to a dear friend who is going to carry out your wishes. But first, he must know what these wishes are. If you are looking for a mineral deposit, tell this to your low self. Tell it that you want it to work with Lady Luck to find a mineral deposit for you. Whatever it is that you are looking for, be as explicit as you can in telling the low self to find it for you.

If you want to locate a treasure, but not a specific one, tell your low self that you want to discover a treasure of great value to you. Ask it to work with Lady Luck to find it and tell you where it is. It will be difficult to say what kind of treasure you will get without telling your low self exactly what it is that you want. It might be fun to do this and see what you come up with. The important thing in giving instructions to the low self is to be sure it understands *what* you really want. So you must be sure you have definite ideas of what you want.

B. Build a Force Field of Mana

Here, as in other rituals, you are going to build a powerful force field of mana so that your command will have authority and strength. In this case, you are going to impart some of this power to Lady Luck so she can do what you ask her.

1. Take six deep breaths, holding each as long as you can before taking the next one.
2. After three breaths, hold your hands out in front of you, palms facing. Feel the Mana-Force build as you take the remaining three deep breaths.
3. Be still for a few moments and feel the Power you have generated.

C. Give Your Command

Now you will use the tremendous Power and "livingness" of the concentrated Mana-Force Power to direct and energize Lady Luck. Give the following command in a strong authoritative voice:

> *Lady Luck, I* command *you to work with my low self*
> *to find the treasure I have asked for. I* command
> *you to let me know where it is. I* command *this*
> *with my full heart and soul. It* is *done. So* be *it.*

HOW JED F. TURNED A FISHING TRIP
INTO A FORTUNE WITH THE USE OF
MANA-FORCE POWER

Just because Jed F. turned a fishing trip into a fortune doesn't mean that we should all dash out to go fishing. His fortune came from Mana-Force Power and Lady Luck. The use of these two Powers I do recommend to everyone.

The man I shall call Jed had studied and used Mana-Force Power for several years before the events of this story occurred. At first, he had limited its use to things of a nonmaterial nature, such as gaining release from Karmic debts, improving his relations with others, finding peace within, and so on. Now he was interested in finding out what he could accomplish with Mana-Force Power in the sense of material wealth.

Jed had laid his plans carefully. He had arranged to take his annual vacation in October, and for this he had reserved a houseboat on the waterways of the delta in Central California. He would drive to the marina and then spend three weeks on the water. He wanted to be as relaxed as possible while he explored the Mana-Force Power ritual for finding treasure.

His planning paid off well. In just a few days, he was completely at home on the boat. The weather was perfect and the fishing was all anyone could ask for. Now that he was settled in he was ready to perform the ritual. He decided that early the next morning would be a suitable time.

Just before sunrise Jed seated himself on the deck and watched the countryside come to life. There was a slight haze over the water that gave an unreal beauty to the scene. He felt that there could be no better setting for his purpose.

As soon as he had completed the reveal-treasure-to-me ritual, he knew he had reached the most powerful level he had ever experienced. Now he would await the results with interest.

Approximately twenty-four hours later, Jed knew that he had indeed been successful. There was no doubt about it.

Quite early the next morning after performing the ritual, he started up a small stream on a fishing trip. He had traveled a mile or so in his inflatable boat when he came to an ideal fishing spot. The stream widened to form a large pool. Jed knew that this would be an ideal haunt for bass. He beached his boat and prepared the tackle.

Less than two hours later, he had his limit of exceptionally large fish. As he was sitting on a fallen log, he again thought of the treasure ritual of the day before. "Maybe the exceptional fish are my treasure," he thought. "They certainly are the most impressive I've seen." He thought that unless something better came along, he could give credit for the fish to Lady Luck.

Then, just as he was about to leave, he noticed something flash in the water. Thinking it might be a lost lure, he lay down on the bank and reached for the object. But he couldn't quite reach it from the bank. He decided to let it go.

He walked to his boat and prepared to return to the houseboat. As soon as he headed the little rubber boat toward home, a very strange thing happened to Jed. His skin began to tingle and a bright light seemed to flash in his mind. In a few seconds, it seemed like the flashing was coming from under water. Then he realized it was the same thing he had seen a few minutes before. At the same time, he felt a desire to find the source of the flashes.

Turning the boat around, he paddled to where he had first seen the glint of the sun on an object. Yes, there it was again, a golden glitter, just as before. Reaching into the water he picked up the object. At first he didn't know what the small, odd-shaped form was. Slowly it dawned on him what he had found. It was a sizable gold nugget. Jed didn't know much about gold but he knew that a piece this size would be very valuable.

He put the nugget in his tackle box. Then he stretched out, face down, and started going over the bottom of the stream. For fifteen minutes he found nugget after nugget. Then he could find no more.

He stopped and looked at what he had found. There were two large handfuls of the golden treasure. Again Jed searched the bottom, but it was evident that there were no more nuggets there. Later during his stay, Jed returned to the same spot to search again. But he found no more gold.

At the end of his vacation, Jed stopped in San Francisco to get an appraisal of his gold. He told the assayer where he had found the nuggets. The man said that gold had never been found in that particular area before. It looked like a small earthquake must have exposed a gold deposit in the stream bed.

Then he told Jed the good news. He said the gold Jed found was worth more than $6,000 on the world market. He also thought that, as nuggets, the gold was worth possibly $12,000 if sold to nugget collectors. After all, these were all sizable nuggets.

Well, this was one vacation trip that really paid off. The circumstances surrounding his find of the nuggets informed Jed that the beautiful fish he caught were not the only result of the reveal-treasure-to-me ritual he had used!

POWER-POINTERS

1. Don't implore but COMMAND Lady Luck to reveal hidden treasure and fabulous fortune to you!

2. Study the *Questions* and *Answers* in this Power chapter to see how others like yourself have been taught the secrets of Power.

3. Remember: Lady Luck *has* to obey you if you command her in authoritative language.

4. Concentrate on the Morris Plan for giving instructions to the low self, building Mana-Force Power, and sending your commands.

5. Write out your wishes and practice commands until you *become* confident, certain, and authoritative!

6. Make Mana-Force Power yours and make the rituals work for you, too!

Editor's Note on Power #6

We are told in the Bible that we are made in the image of God. This means that we, too, can create with the use of the Power Word—spoken with authority!

God did not say, "Please, let there be light" or "Oh, how I wish it were light." He *commanded*: "LET THERE BE LIGHT!" And there was light and it was good. You can create the same way.

A series of vibrations are set up when you speak the Powerful Word. When these vibrations are strong enough, they can travel great distances and affect many other people. With the titanic Mana-Force Power you will propel your Word into the ethers with the force of a rocket-thrust, and Lady Luck will do your bidding!

Follow all instructions in this chapter faithfully and you will be amazed to find that you are actually and magically using the magnificent Mana-Force Power of Hawaii.

The next exciting and life-enhancing Power to be added to your remarkable Treasury of occult and mystic Powers is the tremendous AVATAR POWER that will bring health, wealth and happiness *flooding* to you!

POWER 7

the titanic new avatar power rituals that bring health, wealth and happiness flooding to you

NAP—The Tremendous Manipulative Force
That Compels Miracles to Happen For You

$t$his Power is one of the most dynamic additions to your growing Treasury of Occult and Mystic Powers. It is based upon the remarkable findings of Occultist Geof Gray-Cobb, whose psychic investigations unearthed the secret as revealed in his book, *The Miracle of New Avatar Power*. This incredible Power is now yours!

"Once you use this practical method," says this Master Mystic, "you can renew your body and transform your entire environment. The Powers you are bending to your will are those that keep the Wheels of the Universe circulating smoothly."

By adhering to the expert instructions provided by Gray-Cobb in what follows you will bring this amazing Power to bear in your own life.

MASTER MYSTIC KEY

The primary step is to feel this Power flowing close to you from an inexhaustible reservoir. Next, you bring the Power to a peak. Then you locate five major centers in and around your body. These centers are the gates to the Power that is waiting to pour into your being.

You will remember that Power #2 introduced you to Vital Centers and Chakras (review that chapter at your leisure). This has "tilled the ground" of your psyche so that now your Mind can assimilate the powerful truth about your Five New Avatar Power Gates.

To open these Gates you must use five Arcane Names of Invocation, and these are provided for you. As you begin the Ritual below and recite the Names, you will thrill to the feeling of the Power pouring through your body and outward into your environment to change all your circumstances and situations *for your benefit*.

You will now learn to focus this Power with an ancient Ritual and its accompanying Words of Power.

HOW TO MANIPULATE THE POWER THAT COMPELS MIRACLES TO HAPPEN TO YOU

The picture of the male in Figure 1 looks rather as if he is standing behind a pole with five balloons inflated around it. In

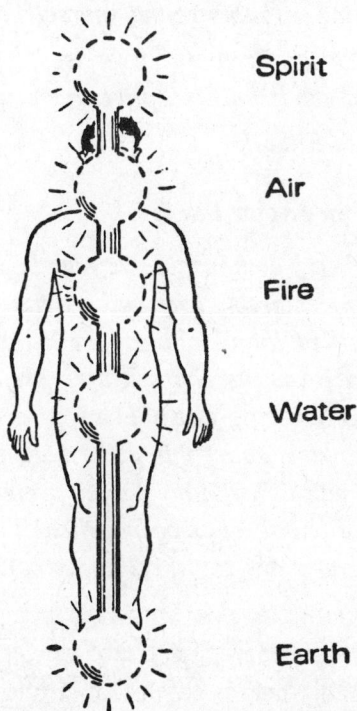

Spirit

Air

Fire

Water

Earth

Figure 1: The Five New Avatar Power Gates

actual fact, this is how you are going to pretend you are as you usher in the awesome flow of your NAP.

Notice that the five "balloons" are labeled Earth, Water, Fire, Air, and Spirit, from the feet to the head. These are traditional names for the five gates through which your New Avatar Power (NAP) is going to cascade.

These gates are almost always totally closed, but the Rituals you have already been given have opened some of the gates. The Ritual that follows will open the gates fully, flooding you with crackling Power.

HOW TO PERFORM THE RITUAL FOR OPENING THE NEW AVATAR POWER GATES

1. *Get familiar with the picture in Figure 1. Imagine the Five Gates existing invisibly round yourself, as in the picture.*
2. *Do some "Prana Breathing Exercises," as in Power #2 to get yourself ready and receptive to Occult Forces. Then,*
3. *Perform this Ritual:*

Bringing in Your New Avatar Power

Make yourself very comfortable in your bed or favorite chair. Imagine NAP flowing smoothly over and around you. Feel it traveling upwards to the "balloon" above your head. When you reach this point, start to open the Spirit Gate. Pretend that a white, sparkling balloon is hovering just above your scalp.

As you are thinking about this white ball, pretend that it has become a ball of white light. Many people pretend that an electric light bulb inside the balloon has been switched on.

As the light comes on, say the First Arcane Word of Power: "EH-HEH-YEH."

That's easy to say. The vowels are short, so that the three sounds of the Word all rhyme with "Oh, yeah!"

Slowly repeat the Word of Power a total of three times as you let the idea of the ball of white light grow in your mind. You will begin to feel a prickling sensation in your fingers and toes.

Now pretend that a round white shaft of light, about three inches thick, is moving out from the lower side of the ball of light. That shaft moves slowly down through your skull until it reaches your throat. This is the Air Gate.

Pretend that a second ball of white light is growing in your throat, opening up and spreading out until it covers your neck, jaws and eyes. You pretend that your head, up as far as your eyebrows, is inside the ball of light.

Say the Second Arcane Word of Power: "YEH-HO-VO-EL-OH-HEEM."

Pronounce the "Yeh" as in the First Word; "Ho" is just the same as Santa Claus's "Ho! HO! HO!"; "Vo" rhymes with "Ho"; "El" is said like the letter L; "Oh" like "I owe you a nickel"; and "Heem" rhymes with "team."

Say the Word three times in all and feel your throat begin to glow and tingle.

Pretend that the shaft of light now thrusts on down through your chest to the Fire Gate, on a level with your heart. Pretend that a third ball of light expands within your chest, extending from the front of your body through to the back.

Say the Third Arcane Word of Power: "YEH-HO-VO-EL-OG-VE-DAH-AS."

The first five syllables are exactly the same as those of the Second Word; then "Ve" rhymes with "pay"; "Dah" rhymes with "far"; and "As" rhymes with "pass."

Say the Word twice more, and feel a warmth spreading through your chest cavity.

Pretend that the shaft of light is now thrusting on down to the Water Gate which is located at your genitals. Pretend that a ball of white light expands through your body in that position as you say the Fourth Arcane Word of Power: "SHAD-AI-EL-KAI."

"Shad" rhymes with "had"; "Ai" is spoken like the word "eye"; "El" as before; and "Kai" rhymes with "high."

Say the Word twice more, slowly, and experience a comfortable warmth throughout your pelvic region.

Complete this part of the Ritual by pretending that the shaft of light thrusts down between your legs to your feet where a fifth ball of light expands.

Say the Fifth Arcane Word of Power: "AH-DOH-NAI-HA-AH-RETZ." "Ah" as the doctor tells you to "Say Ah!"; "Doh" like a female rabbit, "Doe"; "Nai" to rhyme with "sky"; "Ha" rhymes with "far"; "Ah" the same as the first one; and finally, "Retz" rhymes with "bets." Say the Word twice more slowly.

The picture you have in your mind's eye should be a shaft of fiery white light running from your head to your toes, inside your body, studded with five gigantic, brilliant white gems—three along the center and one at each end.

You are now fully charged with raw NAP and your final tasks are to circulate it and then direct it to carry out its miraculous purposes in your life.

OCCULTOMATIC POWER STIMULATOR

Are you short of money? Does your love-life disappoint you? Are you a victim of poor health? Is the world against you? Do you feel that you are in a rut from which you may never escape? Does day-to-day living frustrate and annoy you? Do you seek power over your enemies? Is there anything about your life which you would like to change?

If your answer is "Yes" to any of the above questions, you are in the right place at the right time! Your New Avatar Power can alter your whole existence for the better. Whatever your particular problem, practice the above Gate-Opening Ritual. Then, in time of need and for quick help, stimulate your new Power in this manner:

The New Avatar Power Circulation Ritual

1. *As you lie or sit, fully charged with NAP, take the next step toward sending your NAP streaming out to do your bidding*

2. *Bring your attention to the Spirit Gate, where you have created the ball of white light above your head. Pretend that the light turns to a liquid stream and begins to flow down the left side of your body, painting your left shoulder, arm, hip, leg, and foot with white brilliance. As you imagine this downflow, breathe out slowly at your normal, relaxed speed.*

3. *When the stream of light reaches the ball of light corresponding to the Earth Gate at your feet, begin to breathe in slowly, and pretend that the stream of light is running up the right side of your body, back to the ball of light at the Spirit Gate. On the way up it bathes your right leg, hip, arm, and shoulder with sparkling brilliance, just as it did to your left side on the way down.*

4. *Perform this imaginary circulation, down on the left and up on the right, as you take five more deep and easy breaths.*

5. *Now you add a second flow to the first. In time with an outgoing breath, pretend that the light from the Spirit Gate is flowing down the front of your body, bathing your face, chest, stomach, thighs, legs, and feet in brilliance.*

6. *Then, as you inhale, imagine the flow sweeping under your feet and up at the back of your body, flooding white light over your calves, buttocks, back, shoulders, and neck.*

7. *Repeat this second flow five times, breathing in rhythm with the down and up motion of this waterfall of imaginary light.*

8. *You have now imagined yourself to be inside a flowing, circulating stream of New Avatar Power.*

QUESTIONS AND ANSWERS ABOUT THE
MIRACLE-WORKING NEW AVATAR POWER

Question: *Exactly what* is *New Avatar Power?*
Answer: Quite simply, it is what the Ancient Egyptians, the Essenes, and many other ancient races of men used to call "The Power of the Mysteries." It is the same Power that was sought in the Middle Ages by witches, warlocks, sorcerers, theurgists, and alchemists.

Question: *Then NAP can be used in magical ways?*
Answer: The results you get are certainly *like* magic! Power, money, love, health—your New Avatar Power will give them all to you.

Question: *I seem to be feeling listless lately. Can New Avatar Power give me some energy?*
Answer: You bet! Mike P. was 65 years old and feeling rundown and finished with life. He opened his five Power gates and regained vitality and vigor.

Question: *Ever since I was a little girl I've dreamed of miracles happening in my life. How can I get them to really happen?*
Answer: As in every other endeavor, practice makes perfect. Your question reminds me of a young woman I know in Brooklyn. Her name is Wendy. She was an unemployed go-go dancer, actually on the verge of suicide, she was so downcast and pessimistic. A miracle like you speak of occurred in her life and turned it completely around. She had been practicing New Avatar Power Rituals and one day, quite unexpectedly, a very wealthy man appeared on her doorstep, looking for her. He had seen her perform her dances and had fallen in love with her. It so happened that he appeared in her life just when she needed help badly. Wendy is now the lady of the house in an extravagant Southern mansion. A retinue of servants attend to her tiniest needs. She takes world trips with her handsome new husband. She is paradisiacally happy. You can be, too!

WHAT *DO* YOU WANT NEW AVATAR POWER
TO BRING YOU?

Right now, make a clear and concise statement which indicates your most heartfelt wish. In quite clear language, so your subconscious mind understands, say:

Within the very next week I sincerely want —————. (Complete the statement in your own words.)

It is important that you know precisely what you want out of life. Make a list of goals, wishes, dreams, needs. Each week complete the above statement with one of them and WORK AT IT!

Once you have clearly formulated your desires, New Avatar Power will come to your aid if you obey the instructions given.

With your desire planted firmly in your heart and mind, practice the foregoing Ritual. Get your New Avatar Power *flowing*!

Then perform the following amazing Ritual:

THE NEW AVATAR POWER FOUNTAIN RITUAL

1. *After taking the twelve breaths and imagining the circulation of your NAP, think about the ball of light at the Earth Gate at your feet. Recall the shaft of light that you pretended was thrusting through the other balls of light.*

2. *Imagine that the Spirit Gate has turned into a powerful suction pump which is sucking the white light from the Earth Gate and up the center shaft. Inhale as you pretend that the light is rising in the shaft.*

3. *Then pretend that the light bursts out of the top of the shaft like a brilliant fountain. Begin to exhale, and imagine the light showering down all over you from the Spirit Gate over your head.*

4. *Take five more deep breaths, sucking the light up the shaft and then imagining it cascading down your body like a waterfall, to be absorbed again by the ball of light at your feet.*

5. *You will now feel your NAP physically. With your body relaxed and still, a great calmness will surge through your mind, while your skin will prickle with warmth and a vibrant current of life.*

6. *Now is the moment to heal any part of your body that needs mending. If a physical disorder has been troubling you, think about the part of your body that is sick. If your normal mental patterns are not as clear-cut as you would wish, direct your attention inside your head.*

7. *You are now overflowing with the Power of NAP and you bring this tide of Power to a foaming, glorious peak by reading the following invocation aloud slowly, with feeling.*

Invocation to Strengthen the Fountain of Your New Avatar Power

Thee I invoke, The Bornless One. Thou are Man made perfect, whom no man has seen at any time. This is He whom the winds fear. Hear me, and make all subject unto me, so that every spell and scourge of the Vast One shall be made obedient to me.

I am He, the Bornless Spirit, strong and of immortal fire. I am He, the Truth, that lighteneth and thundereth. I am He whose mouth ever flameth. I am He the begetter and manifester unto the Light.

These words have a Mystic Power of their own. They are a true Invocation to Hidden Spiritual Beings, and they have been used by powerful adepts for centuries. By saying the words, you are attuning yourself with the Power of those adepts, and the still greater Powers of the Beings.

If anyone else says these words, nothing will happen. But you, because you are activating the forces of Occult and Mystic Powers,

are in a position to use them for what they actually are—
CREATIVE WORDS OF POWER AND FORCE!

HOW TO USE THE CENTRAL PILLAR RITUAL
TO PERFORM MIRACLES

The whole of the Ritual described so far is known as the Central Pillar Ritual. As you finish reading the invocation, you can proceed directly to the miracle working.

Perhaps there are necessities of life that you need, or maybe some luxury you have been denied. Use your NAP first to bring just what you want to yourself.

Just consider what you desire to have, or what undesirable circumstance you may wish to be rid of. Then add the Power of the Major Planets to bring luxuries flooding to you, or to send the unpleasant parts of your life hurtling out of your affairs forever.

In Figure 2, you will see a table that lists the Seven Major Planets, the subjects those planets control, the banishing and attracting colors associated with each planet, and the Name of the Mystic Being who controls each planet.

Warning: Treat those Names with care. They are ultimately powerful, and should be respected. Keep them secret from people who do not know about NAP. *In particular, refrain from attaching the Names to other people, things, or pets.*

Glance through the list of planetary subjects, searching for what you desire. If you have debts to pay or recover, then Saturn is the planet. If you wish to attract a woman and win her love, the Moon should be used. A requirement for a new television will be satisfied by Mercury. If you desire a luxurious home, a second or third car, a swimming pool, four mink coats, or any other outrageous extravagance, Venus will work that miracle for you.

The only other thing you need to know is that the Attracting Colors bring things *to* you, while the Banishing Colors send things *away* from you, or send them to other people.

PLANET	CONTROLLING SUBJECTS	COLORS		NAME	HOW TO PRONOUNCE THE NAME
		BANISHING	ATTRACTING		
Saturn	Real estate. Agricultural implements. Debts and their repayment. Old people. Furniture. Wills and death. Relatives.	Indigo	Dark Blue	Jehovah Elohim	YEH-HO-VO ELL-OH-HEEM
Jupiter	Gambling. Debtors. Creditors. Bankers. Long journeys. Dreams. Generosity. Growth. Plenty.	Purple	Blue	El	ELL
Mars	Construction. Destruction. Energy. Haste. Anger. Cars and trucks. Danger. Surgery. Vitality. Willpower.	Red	Red	Elohim Gibor	ELL-OH-HEEM GEE-BORE
Sun	Employers. Executive powers. Officials. Power and success. Money. Gold. Life. Health. Mental powers. Growing things.	Orange	Gold	Jehovah Eloah Ve-Daäs	YEH-HO-VO ELL-OH-WUH VAY-DAH-ASS
Venus	Love. Young people. Social affairs. Pleasure. Art. Music. Beauty. Luxury. Self-indulgence. Extravagance.	Jade	Emerald Green	Jehovah Tzavoös	YEH-HO-VO TZAH-VO-OSE
Mercury	Business matters. Writing. Contracts. Short journeys. Buying. Selling. Neighbors. Messages. Books. Papers. Electrical and electronic apparatus and appliances.	Yellow	Orange	Elohim Tzavoös	ELL-OH-HEEM TZAH-VO-OSE
Moon	Women. General public. Removals. Changes. Personality. Ghosts. Spirits. Magic. Boats. Aircraft.	Blue	Puce	Shadai El Chai	SHAH-DYE ELL KIGH

Figure 2: The Seven Major Planets

Thus the blue of Jupiter would help to bring you abundance, while the yellow of Mercury would help you to sell belongings that you no longer need.

So write down your desire in a few words. Then make a note of the name of the appropriate planet and the color you are going to use. Lastly, write the Name of the Mystic Being who controls that planet.

THREE EASY STEPS TO GETTING WHAT YOU DESIRE OUT OF LIFE

1. Study the chart in Figure 2.
2. Perform the whole of the Central Pillar Ritual. In your imagination, you are bathed in Light.
3. Select the Planetary Color appropriate to your desire and miracle and pretend that the white Light is changing to this color.

You are now focusing the Powers of the Universe to bring your desire which you have written down into startling reality.

Mystic Master Geof Gray-Cobb reminds you: "On average, your miracles will occur within seven days of starting the Ritual. Some, however, will occur almost instantaneously, while others may take a little longer."

HOW TO ATTRACT AND BANISH WITH YOUR NEW AVATAR POWER

Obtaining Gold. Let us assume that you desire to receive some gold to boost your bank balance.

Write down: "I wish to receive $10,000 (or whatever amount you wish) worth of gold." Be specific.

Examining the chart in Figure 2, you can see that the Sun is concerned with gold, and to bring it to you, the Sun's attracting color of gold needs to be used.

So write down, "Sun" and "Gold." Lastly, you must write "Jehovah Eloah Ve-Dass."

Perform the Ritual, pretending that the Light around you has turned to bright, sparkling gold as you say the Name of the Mystic Being.

Then, as you sit for a few minutes enjoying the vibrations of the Ritual, pretend that the gold is already cascading into the room, piling up all around you!

Sending a Present to a Friend. Suppose you wish to do a favor for a friend, and arrange for him to receive some books he has said he needs.

Carry out the Ritual, except that you will use the banishing color of Mercury, which governs books. Write down, "Send my friend the books he needs. Mercury. Yellow. Elohim Tzavoös." As you pretend that the light is changing to brilliant yellow, and call three times to Elohim Tzavoös, pretend that someone, anyone, is giving the required books to your friend. He will receive them shortly.

Gaining the Love of a Partner. Producing an abstract benefit, one which you cannot touch and see, is done in much the same way.

The planet Venus is concerned with love and pleasure. The color that will bring love to you is emerald green. So you would write down "I desire a loving partner. Venus. Emerald Green. Jehovah Tzavoös, and carry out the Ritual using that color and those words and Name.

Debt Repayments. Saturn governs debts. If you wish to get out of debt, you should write down "I wish to be free of debt. Saturn. Indigo. Jehovah Elohim."

Note that you use the banishing color, because you want to send the debts away from you.

Notice that while this will make you free of debt, it will not necessarily bring money to you. The result of the Ritual could be that the person to whom you owe money calls you up and says that he has decided to cancel your debt to him for some reason or another.

Removing Undesirable Character Traits. While you are deciding what miracle you wish to work for yourself, you may decide that some part of your character needs changing. Perhaps you realize with a blinding flash that people have been calling you mean and miserable for years.

So you call on the Mystic Being El and the blue attracting color of Jupiter. Your desire would be written down as: "I wish to be generous."

HOW LOUISE K. BANISHED EVIL
INFLUENCES FROM AROUND HER

Louise K. from San Bernardino lived alone. An old woman who lived further down the road had once cursed Louise for some imagined slight.

"Everything I touch crumbles to ashes," Louise wrote to me. "Bad luck haunts me. People stare at me when I go out, and I can hardly sleep for all the strange noises which go on in my house. It's making me a nervous wreck.

"Now my son has run off with some slip of a hippie girl, my husband is dead, I've only got a few dollars welfare coming in and altogether I'm a miserable, penniless old woman."

By mail, I sent her instructions on how to call on Shadai El Chai, using the blue banishing color of the Moon as she performed the NAP Ritual.

"What a relief," she wrote to me two days later. "I slept a full night in my own room last night. All the evil influences have gone. My son came home again this morning. He's left the girl, and he's going to care for me. I'm delighted to get straight so quickly."

CHOOSE YOUR MIRACLE AND WORK IT NOW

A little preliminary work in selecting the correct planet and color will truly work any miracle that you ask for.

Carry out the Ritual, pretending that what you have asked for is rapidly winging towards you, and it will assuredly happen.

You are now fully experienced in the methods of miracle-working. Start at once to change your life, banishing the influences and effects that have been holding you back for so long and making you unhappy. Then start into the joyful task of automatically attracting the luxury and prosperity you have lacked for so long.

You are now using your seventh Power of your Parker Lifetime Treasury of Occult and Mystic Powers. Use it happily, successfully, and with anticipation of desires and wishes fulfilled!

POWER-POINTERS

1. Remember that New Avatar Power (NAP) is an ancient magical Force which you are utilizing for modern, twentieth-century miracle-working in your own personal life.

2. Study Figure 1 until you *know* that you, too, possess the Five Magic Gates of Power.

3. Practice the New Avatar Power Ritual before each and every operation for success and riches.

4. Get clear in your mind what it is you expect of NAP and perform each Ritual carefully.

5. Recite the Invocation to Strengthen the Fountain often, remembering that the words have a Mystic Power of their own.

6. Study the chart in Figure 2 and get familiar with the Planet-Color correspondences. It is good practice to make a list, writing down, "Sun-Gold, Mars-Red, Mercury-Orange, etc."

7. Review the "Three Easy Steps to Getting What You Desire Out of Life," and apply them to each of your wishes.

Editor's Note on Power #7

You will heighten your chances of delightful success if you will get into the habit of writing down your wishes, desires, dreams, and goals. THINK—WRITE—RECEIVE! Graphologists do not speak of "handwriting," but of "brainwriting," for they know that when one writes something down, it is the brain using the hand as a tool. Become conscious of this psychological fact. Think of what you want, write it down, make a list—and then *act* by employing your new occult Power.

Observe some person who is "down-and-out" and you will see a person who lacks personal Power. Don't let life or Fate batter you about like a leaf in the wind—get smart! Study, review, and absorb the secrets of your occult and mystic Powers.

You have already been faithfully recording and noting primary portions of your Power chapters. It is wise to go back every few days and see if other sentences, clues, keys or revelations ask for your attention. Copy them, word for word, in your Personal Power Notebook.

> The next Power in your Treasury reveals a startling secret of Hypnosis, shared with you by two eminent hypnologists—an easy six-step program for turning your idle fancies into happy facts!

power 8

how to enjoy achievement power through hypno-cybernetics

The Six-Step Program That Virtually Guarantees Achieving Your Goals

"Great minds have purposes," remarked Washington Irving, "others have wishes."

The noted British prime minister, Benjamin Disraeli, added, "The secret of success is constancy to purpose."

This chapter translates wishes into specific purposes—goals that can be automatically programmed for attainment.

Then you are assured "constancy to purpose" by programming yourself to keep on the track, step after accomplished step.

This is Hypno-Cybernetics at its fulfilling best.

MASTER MYSTIC KEY

Like the Intercontinental Ballistics Missile programmed to seek out and arrive at its target, we, too, seem born with an innate fervent desire to reach our goals. Yet many of us spend our lives in a rut, never really enjoying achievement or realizing our highest hopes. In this Power-packed chapter, based on techniques presented in their book *Hypno-Cybernetics*, noted hypnologist Sidney Petrie and Mind-Power specialist Robert B. Stone, provide you with the dynamite Power that will remove the "rut" from your programming and substitute "goal," so you will take off like a missile thrust.

When the missile shoots for its target, it doesn't "know" the target has never been reached before. It doesn't think about it or mull it over or doubt it can be done. It zooms to its destination with inexorable accuracy and speed.

"The same with our subconscious computer," say Petrie and Stone. "Its nervous system, like the electronics system, cannot tell the difference between something programmed to be done for the first time or something programmed to be done for the millionth time. It's just as automatic for it to make you head of the firm you have been working for as to wake you up at 6:30 a.m. for the thousandth time."

What desire would you like to have fulfilled? What do you need to brighten your life? What would you like to be? Where would you like to go? How rich would you like to be?

Set your goal—the target—and let Hypo-Cybernetics (H-C) project you right to it!

THE MAGIC POWER OF PRETENDING

In the last chapter you learned (among other marvelous things) how to pretend that you are surrounded by glorious white Light. When you pretend with *Power*, you create!

"How can I see myself getting a pay raise when salaries are being cut?"

"Can you pretend you are getting the pay raise?"

"Well, sure, I can pretend, but where's that going to get me?"

IT GOT HIM A BIG, FAT BONUS!

A woman in Albany, New York was having a great deal of difficulty with a particularly vicious neighbor with whom she could not contend.

"She's too evil for me," she said.

"Well, then overcome her with Good. Pretend your subconscious did it."

The pretense worked! The neighbor couldn't move away from the community fast enough! After just a few sessions, her trouble was over, and she was getting excellent H-C results.

THE POWER OF CONTROLLED IMAGINATION

With the Power of Hypno-Cybernetics (H-C), you soon learn to control your imagination to bring you amazing and delightful results in whatever you undertake. Many a Power Pretender to riches and success has achieved his wishes, desires, and goals in this life. Pretend, and you *become*. Here is why:

Imagine you are unwrapping a thick steak. You are setting it into a red-hot frying pan. Can you hear it sizzle? Does your mouth water? Chances are you have had to swallow as the saliva flowed, just imagining a sizzling steak.

> Pretending triggers the imagination.
> Imagination creates behavior.
> Behavior forms habits.

These three steps happen every day to every human being, whether they know it or not. It is automatic. Unfortunately, many people think they are failures and proceed to live up to their self-image in their imagination. Then they behave like a failure and get the failure-habit.

You can turn it all around.

Pretend you are a millionaire, or a great lover, or a business success. Will such pretending bring you what you want out of life? YES—if you apply the Power of Hypno-Cybernetics as directed by Petrie and Stone!

QUESTIONS AND ANSWERS ABOUT THE
SUCCESS POWER OF H-C

Question: Exactly how does H-C work to create miracles?

Answer: Take a look at the word Hypno-Cybernetics. You see it is a combination of two words—the prefix for "hypnotism" and "cybernetics." Hypnotism is the modern means we have to contact a large portion of our mind called the subconscious or automatic mind. Cybernetics is the equally modern means we have to instruct or program any automated device. So Hypno-Cybernetics is a modern means to contact our vast subconscious mind and program it to do our bidding.

Question: What makes you think I can benefit from Hypno-Cybernetics?

Answer: The authors of H-C are paramedics. That is to say, they work under the auspices of physicians or psychiatrists where weight loss, cigarette smoking, fears and phobias, or other health factors are involved. With or without the health factor, it is important to acknowledge one thing: Hypno-Cybernetics works! It does not matter that *we* think H-C will benefit you; but it is absolutely vital that *you* think so.

Question: I need some new clothes. My wife needs extra spending money. The house needs repair. My kids can use a few luxuries, Ned a car, Susie a bike. How do I go about getting the cash for these things?

Answer: Your mind is wonderful, the way it works. We all want to have enough money for food, housing, bills, travel, and some left over for luxuries. Know that it can be. *The mind does it all.* It can be programmed for unending money troubles or good fortune after good fortune. And Hypno-Cybernetics is the way to program your mind for whatever you want out of life.

Start right now to digest the Petrie and Stone H-C Six-Step Program to Better Living.

THE SIX EASY STEPS TO THE POWER
OF HYPNO-CYBERNETICS

Write down, study, and memorize these six vital steps:

1. Plan
2. Accept
3. Practice
4. Reinforce
5. Apply
6. Expect

I. *Plan*

Some people hitch their wagons to a star. Your goal does not have to be sky high. Begin by using your new Power for the attainment of a modest goal, such as:

*Finding a marriage partner in the next year.

*Purchasing your own home within six months.

*Getting a fat pay raise in the next 30 days.

*Turning your natural talent into cold hard cash before the year is out.

*Overcoming all setbacks and evil influences within six months.

*Being an "A" student this year.

*Winning a Big-Money contest within 18 months.

Sky high or hedge high, your goal will be reached.

Note that all the goals listed above include a time limit. You need to program a time factor into your automatic mind. How else will it know when to perform? A no-time-limit goal is no goal at all.

Set a goal in your mind's eye. Then get ready to enjoy a minute or two of fun. Sit back. Relax. Close your eyes. And visualize your goal as *already reached*. Pretend it is real. See the details of your dream or wish. If the deadline was a year (for example), imagine a calendar with the set date on it.

Pretend your goal is reached . . . See it . . . Sense it . . . Take it all in . . . Create the details . . . Know it is so . . . Enjoy it . . . Act it out in your imagination—with Power!

II. *Accept*

You have a *plan*. You are programmed to reach for it. You must now *accept* its attainment.

What is really happening is that your automatic mind is concentrating all your natural talent, creativity, knowledge, and intuition on your goal. You are being moved in its direction, effortlessly.

Remember, this does not happen without "acceptance." Here is how to program yourself through that second step:

> I accept this goal as natural and right for me. It is the
> life-style I desire. It is me being myself, expressing my
> true nature. I aim for it. I reach for it.

III. *Practice*

Your goal is etched into your automatic mind.

Acceptance of this goal has started your motor.

Now you are ready to practice. Practice in visualizing goal after goal. Take 30 seconds to visualize another goal, desire, wish or dream. Then another—and another. Practice empowering yourself with the amazing force of H-C.

You may not be able to look ahead more than one goal at a time. But as each goal is realized, you will become aware of the next. This will sound familiar to mountain climbers.

And just like a mountain climber, you will enjoy the view from the top.

IV. *Reinforcement*

You are now an experienced H-C programmer. You have a sophisticated mental computer that can handle any program you give it.

You can see how others need to program themselves out of "I can't" attitudes. You can see how others need to program themselves with a better self-image. You can see how others think in terms of failure, obstacles, and pitfalls.

You have been there, too. But you are not there now. You have programmed yourself to see the glass as half full, not half empty. You see yourself with unlimited potential. You no longer think in terms of obstacles. You think in terms of challenges and success.

However, the environment is still throwing brickbats at you. You are still hearing negative programming, possibly from your mate, your friends, your teachers, your co-workers.

You need to reinforce your positive programming. You do this three ways:

1. You reinforce your insulation against negative suggestions from the outside.

2. You strengthen your own positive suggestions for goal attainment.

3. You insure your success by programming yourself to fight for goal attainment.

And here's how:

1. Say: "I am not affected by failure thoughts of others. Negativity bounces off me. Positivity I accept."

2. Strengthen your positive suggestions by writing out a whole list of lovely, exciting goals to be reached.

3. This is a self-administered pep-talk: "Okay, I'm going into the fray with purpose and determination. I'm giving it everything I have!"

Do all three steps often!

V. *Apply*

Apply is the fifth of your six steps. Apply what? Apply yourself?

"That's the old way," say Petrie and Stone. "Hard work, sweat, long hours. That's the physical energy way. Hypno-

Cybernetics is the new way. It offers you the life energy to apply yourself. No sweat. It's like applying your foot to the gas pedal—for increased acceleration.''

Suppose you were to take your eyes off this page and look at the ceiling, close your eyes, and visualize yourself moving toward your goal. What do you see yourself doing? Try it.

Did you come up with something? Move to another city? Buy some new clothes? Win the heart of that lovely girl? Invite the boss to dinner? Win a contest?

Jot down the ideas you came up with. *Apply* your new Power!

VI. *Expect*

The goal you set now may seem too bold, even unrealistic. But you have a powerful ally working for you. H-C will take you there faster than you think.

Expect. Expect to get there with each and every goal you set. Expect some progress every week. Expectation primes your mind. It reminds your brain-computer that you are awaiting results. And it responds!

You can also program your automatic mind to create in you an expectant attitude:

I expect results. I expect progress whether I can see it or not. My expectations are high.

Expect a miracle! Expect to see yourself getting everything that you wish and that you program yourself for. Do the first programming of the Plan, Accept it, and Practice it visually as you read this chapter so that you can be assured you are on your way.

Set new goals and create miracles in your life.

OCCULTOMATIC POWER STIMULATOR

Re-programming the automatic mind is not done with punched tape-like computers. It is done with mental images. Any mental image works, but Hypno-Cybernetic images work best. You can see for yourself how mental images produce what they picture. Try this.

Sit comfortably, close your eyes, see yourself studying the next Power in your Treasury. See yourself interested, absorbed, and convinced that here are the answers for your own life. See yourself doing each exercise called for.

And see yourself reaping a harvest of joy!

HOW J.D. SAVED HIS FAILING BUSINESS

J.D. had a hardware store. Hardware stores were no longer making out. J.D. saw the handwriting on the wall. He knew he had to switch. He heard of other hardware stores taking on small household appliances—electric hair driers, kitchen blenders, clocks, coffee makers, waffle irons, barbeques, and the like.

He invited appliance dealers to send their salesmen. But when the salesmen arrived, he turned the same deaf ear to them as he had been turning to the diehards who kept trying to sell him kegs of nails and other hardware that he couldn't sell.

J.D. was not accepting his own idea. He needed to program himself that it was an idea worth moving ahead on. He used H-C to do this. It wasn't long before the screw bins moved out, the newest in labor-saving appliances moved in, and the customers rediscovered the store.

People who don't accept their own goals are constantly programming themselves not to act. It does not matter what the reason is. It all adds up to zero.

They see "I can." Then they say "I can't." And their automatic mind reports, "Does not compute."

Once you program yourself to *accept* your goal, something quite important happens to your behavior. It begins to evidence "inner drive."

Inner drive puts you in the driver's seat. It gets you where you want to go.

To others it looks as if you are expending a great deal of energy, as if you have an overactive thyroid. Only you are "in" on the secret.

POWER-POINTERS

Remember Disraeli's words of wisdom: "The secret of success is constancy to purpose."

Study your Master Mystic Key and realize the similarity between computerized missiles and your subconscious mind.

Set your goal—the target—and let Hypno-Cybernetics project you right to it!

Reconsider all you have been taught about pretending and remember: Pretending *plus* occult and mystic Power equals SUCCESS!

Review the three steps of Imagination-Behavior-Forming of Habits. Become *conscious* of this Mind Power.

Begin using your new Power of Hypno-Cybernetics by writing down—right now!—at least six immediate goals in your Personal Power Notebook.

1. ....
2. ....
3. ....
4. ....
5. ....
6. ....

Study and practice Petrie and Stone's six-step program for success-building through H-C.

Editor's Note on Power #8

Get to know yourself. Think of the negative things in your life which you want corrected, as well as of the positive things you desire. De-program the negativity; program the positivity.

In your Personal Power Notebook, fill in the following dual list:

	De-Program	*Program*
1.	————————	————————
2.	————————	————————
3.	————————	————————
4.	————————	————————
5.	————————	————————

Check yourself on underlining key phrases in the text. Often a word or two will trigger your new Power—and the same word or two can do this again and again.

The next potent Power to be added to your private Treasury is the Power of Amulets and Talismans, provided for you here from the secret annals of White Witchcraft by the famed occultist Al G. Manning. "The Ceremonial Magic of White Witchcraft," says this noted authority on the subject, "can harness tremendous occult Power— literally invincible Power—to bring you personal benefits of any kind. Invisible, but very real forces will protect you from harm and open the doors of success to your every goal. And because they are part of the Law of the Universe, they cannot refuse to serve you!"

YOUR PARKER PROSPERITY PROGRESS REPORT #2

As with the first Parker Prosperity Progress Report, this Report at the two-thirds point in your Parker Lifetime Treasury of Occult and Mystic Powers is designed to:

1. Give you a breather before going on to more exciting and miracle-working Powers.
2. Give you the opportunity to check on your progress so far.
3. Reinforce your growing ability to *apply* your new Powers.

Instructions:

Each of the following questions is to be answered *Yes* or *No* in your Personal Power Notebook. Remember that this is *your* private record and *your* accumulation of life-enriching information.

Your first Progress Report dealt with the first four chapters of your Treasury; this Report concerns itself with the four Powers you have just completed studying.

Each of your answers is worth 2 points. Your score will reveal your Progress in Power. Do not be concerned if you get more wrong than right; this simply means that the occult and mystic Powers are still taking hold in your mind. Less than 25 wrong answers indicates you are doing well. More than 25 wrong answers means you require further study of each Power. Either way you come out ahead!

Sit comfortably now and turn your attention to what you have learned from your last four Powers and answer these questions. On a blank piece of paper in your Personal Power Notebook, make a listing from 1-26 and write your answer alongside.

1. You can use magic spells to change your luck, increase your wealth, and generally enrich your entire life?
2. Does scientific logic explain magic?
3. Is the Bring-Me-Wealth spell easy to perform?
4. Is a glass of water part of the paraphernalia used in are present?
5. Can other minds interfere with your Cosmic connection?
6. Do you have to be specific when casting a magic spell?
7. When performing the Bring-Me-Wealth spell should you repeat the Ritual 3 times?
8. Does the mystic Power of the Sun play any part in the Win-It-All spell?
9. Is your Lucky Number a number you like best?
10. Should you try to possess the attributes of people you admire?
11. Is a glass of water part of the paraphernalia used in the Young-Again spell?
12. Are your new Powers the same as the Forces of Creation?
13. Did Ben and Karen T. of Topeka, Kansas succeed when they employed Mana-Force?
14. Is the Power to command Lady Luck called Mana-Force Charmetrics?
15. Is a Familiar always wicked?

16. Will indecision weaken the commands you give to Lady Luck?

17. Do you need a bona fide map in order to locate hidden treasure?

18. Is it wise to have definite ideas about what you want before performing magic spells?

19. Is it true that you can build a Force Field of Mana in just three steps?

20. Did Jed F.'s fishing trip turn into a defeat?

21. When you wish something from Lady Luck is it a good habit to beg her with sincerity?

22. Does Lady Luck have to obey you if you use authoritative language?

23. Should you write out wishes and practice commands until you become proficient?

24. Since we are made in the image of God, does this mean we are co-creators with God?

25. Is Mana-Force available to anyone?

26. Are there any rituals connected with New Avatar Power?

27. Is it true that New Avatar Power can open five Power gates in you?

28. Should you do breathing exercises to get yourself ready and receptive to Occult Forces?

29. Is it unwise to get comfortable when doing occult and mystic exercises?

30. Does "NAP" mean "Negative and Positive"?

31. Can you imagine yourself to be inside a flowing, circulating stream of Power?

32. Is the ancient "Power of the Mysteries" the same as New Avatar Power?

33. Can New Avatar Power imbue you with energy even though you are tired and listless?

34. It isn't necessary to repeat Rituals more than once, is it?

35. Should you perform Rituals and Spells alone?
36. Is there such a thing as a Ritual or Invocation to strengthen your occult and mystic Powers?
37. Are Planet vibrations important in performing New Avatar Power Rituals?
38. Is it dangerous to use ancient magical Powers in the twentieth-century?
39. Can you get what you want out of life in just three easy steps?
40. Should you avoid putting your wishes and goals in writing?
41. Do you need to be a qualified hypnotist before you use the Power of Hypno-Cybernetics?
42. Is your subconscious mind like a computer?
43. You should give up pretending if you are going to enjoy riches. Right?
44. Does pretending trigger the imagination?
45. Does imagination create behavior?
46. Are these the Six Steps to Goal-Achievement in Hypno-Cybernetics: Plan, Accept, Practice, Reinforce, Apply, Expect?
47. Does mental imagery play a role in the re-programming of your automatic mind?
48. Isn't it best to have some money in the bank before using Hypno-Cybernetics?
49. Is the secret of success "constancy to purpose?"
50. If you are going to benefit from this book you should refrain from writing in it. Right?

Here's How to Chart Your Progress:

The following questions should have been answered *No:* 2, 4, 9, 15, 17, 20, 21, 29, 30, 38, 40, 41, 43, 48, 50.
All others: *Yes*.
Now score yourself. How did you come out? Better or worse

than your last Progress Report? Let the result determine whether or not you should re-study certain Powers.

If improvement is called for, do not hesitate to go back and study diligently. After all, the only loser is you. And if you develop excellence with your new Powers, you are the only WINNER!

power 9

helping yourself with the pentacle power of white witchcraft

How to Make and Use Amulets, Talismans and Charms for Protection, Mystic Powers and Good Luck

$\mathcal{E}$verything you get in life, you obtain with the help of unseen forces. There is nothing superstitious in this fact. Whether you get what you want from a person, a career or from a "lucky break," the physical manifestation is always accompanied by an unseen, metaphysical quality. You may have a concrete need, but in addition to this need, you exercise a wish, a desire or a dream—the unseen quality.

Have you ever carried a rabbit's foot? A four leaf clover? A St. Christopher's Medal? Did you ever hang a horseshoe over your door? If you spill salt, do you throw some over your left shoulder? How are you on walking under ladders? Our ancestors paid a lot more attention to these things than we "moderns" do, and any good Witch will tell you they were right.

The purpose of this Power chapter, contributed by the famed occultist Al G. Manning, is to explore the protective and "lucky" powers of *things*, which will be used by you to bring you what you need and want out of life.

"Just as candles, incense, herbs and oils add power to your rituals," says Dr. Manning, "so properly consecrated amulets, talismans and charms have Power to influence the unseen side of life to your benefit."

This is why it is wise to bolster your mystic and occult Powers with the secret knowledge of amulets, talismans and charms. Dr. Manning, who here gives you the key to these magical implements from his book *Helping Yourself with White Witchcraft* holds a degree of Master of Religious Science, and is now President of the famous E.S.P. Laboratory in Los Angeles. He provides you with the secrets to working miracles in your life. Follow his advice and instructions in what follows and you will add a potent Power to your growing Treasury.

STONES AND MINERALS FOR YOUR PROTECTION AND GOOD FORTUNE

There is a stone or mineral *meant* for you! Many people are not aware of this mystical Truth. The ancient science of Astrology, as Dr. Manning points out, relates the lucky and protective minerals to the Sign under which you were born. You can find your magical stone by consulting Manning's Table of Stone and Minerals below:

Date of Birth	Your Sun Sign	Lucky and Protective Stones and Minerals	Color
Mar 21/Apr 19	Aries	Diamond, Amethyst, Topaz, Garnet, Iron, Steel	Red
Apr 19/May 20	Taurus	Coral, Sapphire, Emerald, Turquoise, Agate, Zircon, Copper	Azure
May 20/Jun 21	Gemini	Aquamarine, Agate, Amber, Emerald, Topaz, Aluminum	Electric Blue
Jun 21/Jul 22	Cancer	Opal, Pearl, Emerald, Moonstone, Silver	Pearl/Rose
Jul 22/Aug 22	Leo	Diamond, Ruby, Chrysoberyl, Sardonyx, Gold	Orange/Gold

Aug 22/Sep 23	Virgo	Jade, Rhodonite, Sapphire, Carnelian, Aluminum	Gray/Blue
Sep 23/Oct 23	Libra	Opal, Sapphire, Quartz, Jade, Turquoise, Copper	Pale Orange
Oct 23/Nov 22	Scorpio	Bloodstone, Aquamarine, Topaz, Jasper, Silver	Dark Red
Nov 22/Dec 21	Sagittarius	Lapis Lazuli, Topaz, Turquoise, Coral, Tin	Purple
Dec 21/Jan 20	Capricorn	Onyx, Jet, Ruby, Malachite, Lead	Brown
Jan 20/Feb 19	Aquarius	Aquamarine, Jade, Feldspar, Sapphire, Zircon, Aluminum	Green
Feb 19/Mar 21	Pisces	Amethyst, Alexandrite, Bloodstone, Stitchite, Silver	Ocean Blue

Now follow these easy instructions:

1. Find your birthdate or astrological Sign in the above Table and locate your Stone or Mineral.

2. Find or purchase your particular Stone. Do not be concerned if you cannot find yours or if you cannot afford to purchase it. Note the *color* pertaining to you, in such a case, and find a stone of that color and of such a shape that it "feels" right to you.

3. It is important that your Stone be such a size as to fit easily into your hand, pocket or purse.

4. Once you have selected (whether bought or found) the Stone which "appeals" to you, you are ready to consecrate it.

Manning's amazing Consecration Ritual can be performed quickly and easily by anyone. It is designed to amplify the naturally existing "rapport" between you and your amulet.

Get alone with yourself. Sit in a comfortable chair or lie on a bed. Relax. Take a few deep breaths. Then slowly rub your Stone as you recite this chant by Dr. Manning:

MASTER MYSTIC KEY

How to Consecrate Your Lucky Meditation Stone

> Stone of beauty, fine to see,
>> Be consecrated now to me.
> Partners now in growth and life,
>> Helping well in time of strife.
> Tensions strong you take from me,
>> Bring good luck effectively.
> Great amulet for me you'll be,
>> And as my will, so mote it be!

HOW TO USE YOUR CONSECRATED AMULET

You now have in your possession a most personal and potent charm which, given the appropriate condition of your mind, will aid you in every aspect of your life. You have consecrated the Stone and bound it into your personal program of mystic and occult Powers. Keep it with you at all time, in pocket or purse. The more you permit it to feel at one with you, the more positive a "partner" it becomes.

You may use your new Power Amulet for anything you wish. Hold it in your hand and make a wish. Squeeze it and generate strong desire for whatever you need. Whether your need is wealth, health, control over enemies or just good old fashioned fun, your stone will stand you in good stead and will help your dreams come to fruition. It will serve you happily and painlessly as often as you *let* it.

You have now chosen your Stone and consecrated it so that it is your Amulet. So far, so good. Now you want to imbue your Amulet with your own subconscious energy so that it will become a true partner to you. It will become the outer manifestation of your inner powerful being.

To imbue your Amulet with Power you use the Bedtime Ritual as developed by occulist Manning. Choose a Stone that is reasonably flat on at least one side. Then prepare yourself with a bit of scotch tape, a pad of paper and a pencil. That is all you will need.

OCCULTOMATIC POWER STIMULATOR

If your Stone is reasonably small and flat, it can be used to stimulate the creativity and problem-solving ability of your subconscious mind. This technique is highly effective and empowers you to command life.

Simply follow these easy instructions:

1. *When you are ready for bed, bring your Amulet and some scotch tape with you.*

2. *Scotch tape your Amulet to the middle of your forehead.*

3. *Position yourself before a mirror and address your image as if it were your subconscious mind, and instruct it:*

This stone upon my forehead is your reminder of your work for tonight. While the body is asleep, your assignment is to bring the creative solution to my problem of   (whatever it is) When you are ready, wake the body long enough for me to write down the solution, then put it back into a restful, regenerative sleep. Your cooperation will make life more comfortable for the entire organism. Do it!

Make certain that there is a pad of paper and a pencil at your bedside. Then:

4. *Go to sleep knowing that the ritual is working for you.*

5. *When you are awakened with the answer to your problem or the key to your wish, dream or goal, be sure to write it*

down. If you do not, you may suffer the disappointment of realizing that you had the answer last night, but forgot it. Exercise your constructive will with this ritual and make those notes, regardless of the hour or how much you would prefer to stay asleep!

HOW HARRY N. USED THE BEDTIME
AMULET RITUAL TO SOLVE HIS
EMPLOYMENT PROBLEM

Harry N. was given his layoff notice from the junior engineering position he had held for just over a year. There was a brief feeling of despair before he decided to use the technique of programming his subconscious for help. He wasn't quite sure what to ask for, so he kept the instruction general: "Bring me the creative solution to this employment problem."

Harry followed the above steps in your Occultomatic Power Stimulator. During the early hours of the morning, he awakened long enough to sketch an electronic circuit that proved to be an improvement over a subsystem that his ex-employer used in considerable quantity. An enthusiastic trip to the purchasing department convinced the company of significant savings by buying from Harry. And this was the beginning of a successful new electronics firm.

Harry cherishes his Amulet. He was holding it in his hand the day the company gave him his first check—to the amount of $23,000!

FIND OUT WHAT YOU WANT
AND GO AFTER IT!

The following is not a test. It is a self-evaluation chart. Write the answers in your Personal Power Notebook *only*. Just answer *Yes* or *No* to the questions to ascertain in what manner you should immediately use your new Power of Amulet.

I am in desperate need of monetary help.

There is someone channeling negative energy whom I must combat.

I need psychic healing.

There is a particular bill or debt that must be paid.

A certain man (woman) would make my life complete.

I want to win a contest.

A little more fun in life would be good for me.

I am under psychic attack and need powerful aid.

I strongly desire (check one): ( ) a new car; ( ) more love; ( ) a nicer home; ( ) money; ( ) strength to overcome difficulties; ( ) a pay raise; ( ) a new job; ( ) a lucky windfall.

Know what you want! Once you have clearly formulated your desire in your mind, perform the Bedtime Ritual as given above. Tape your magic Amulet to your forehead and speak to your mirrored image as if it were your subconscious mind, and *order* your desire.

A Word of Caution from Manning the Master Mystic: If someone asks to see your Amulet after it has been consecrated to you, the proper reply is: "I'm sorry, but it may not leave my hands." If another person should handle your Amulet, re-consecrate it at the earliest possible moment.

Think of your magic Amulet like your heart. You have probably heard the phrase: "He (or she) is wearing his (or her) heart on his (or her) sleeve." This means that the person in question is open to harm, susceptible to heartbreak. Do not expose your Amulet needlessly. Protect it, and it will protect you. Keep it imbued with *your* psychic energy, not with someone else's. And *treasure* it! It will serve you well.

Study the foregoing portion of this chapter carefully. Get a "feeling" for your Amulet and for the information about it.

Then go on to the next exciting portion which reveals time-honored secrets about Talismans.

QUESTIONS AND ANSWERS CONCERNING
THE MODERN USE OF TALISMANS

Question: What is a Talisman?

Answer: The simplest answer is that a Talisman is a "lucky piece." When you construct a Talisman yourself and wear it on your person or keep it with you at all times, it acts as an attracting force for good and a banishing force for evil.

Question: What can I expect from my Talisman?

Answer: Most people expect and *receive* miracles! This is the whole point of learning occult and mystic Powers: to call down, control and direct unseen Forces. When these supernatural forces are brought into play in your daily life, every aspect of your life is affected for the better.

Question: Don't you have to be an occultist in order to make and use Talismans?

Answer: Absolutely not! You have to be sincere, dedicated, strongly desirous of change, and *expectant*. If you have a particular need to be filled and traditional methods have not worked adequately for you, then mystic and occult forces may very well be the thing for you. Many people secretly turn misery into joy through the use of Talismanic Magic. You can, too!

Question: It all seems so complicated, so ancient and mysterious. How can I take advantage of all these occult secrets?

Answer: By following instructions carefully! Occult Masters have already done all the work *for* you. All you have to do is read, absorb, study, assimilate, and *act* on instructions.

HOW TO AVAIL YOURSELF OF THE POWER
OF TALISMANIC MAGIC

The foregoing chapters of your Treasury of Mystic and Occult Powers has already prepared you for what follows. Your subconscious mind is well tuned to the secrets being revealed here for your benefit. By studying the occult information on Amulets, you set up the vibratory rate required for you to learn about Talismans, Pentacles and—most important of all—Medallions. Magic medallions!

Talismanic Magic has been used for centuries. It dates back to Atlantean times, and you will use this Power *today*. Keep alert. Read carefully. Absorb. And work miracles!

HOW TO HARNESS THE TALISMANIC POWER OF THE SQUARE OF SATURN

From the time of the great King Solomon, the Square of Saturn has been used in magic for protection against enemies—physical and non-physical. This is the way King Solomon himself used it. Figure 3 shows you the complete Pentacle: the Magic Circle of Power.

Now do this:

1. Study the Figure.
2. Do one of three things:
   a. Make your own by having the Square of Saturn stamped on a disc of silver.
   b. Make your own by drawing it with pen and ink on white paper.
   c. Make your own by carefully tracing Figure 3 from this book and pasting in on white paper.

The "do-it-yourself" way of making your own will add more Power to your Pentacles. To harness the Saturnian Power you want a Medallion, one side of which will be your Square of Saturn. We will get to the other side in just a moment. Right now, decide on which way you will make your own Medallion.

HOW TO CONSECRATE YOUR SQUARE OF SATURN

Part of the magic of the *Square of Saturn* is its perfection of form that reads the same from any direction. Set into the Pentacle, as in Figure 3, and properly consecrated, this becomes an exceptionally good protector.

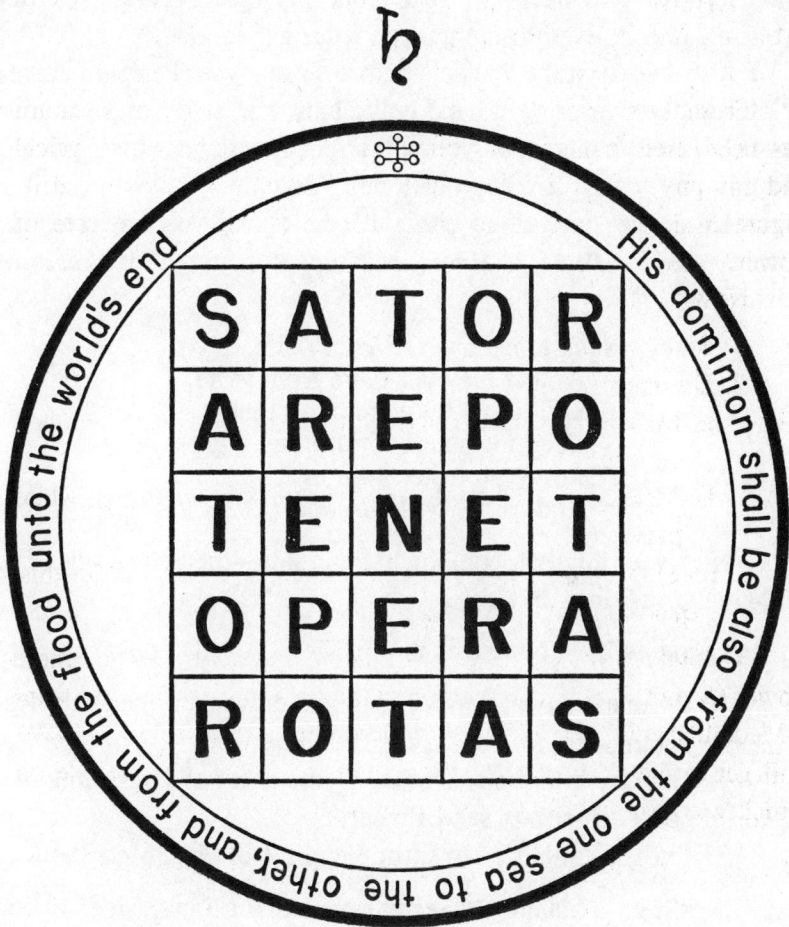

Figure 3: The Square of Saturn as Part of the Pentacle of Saturn

If you make your own with pen and ink, the vibrations from *you* during your loving construction help bind it to you—thus your mood of confidence and peace is essential during the time you are doing your drawing and lettering work. Be neat, but not perfectionist. This will be a *one of a kind* Pentacle because you put yourself into it, even to the uneven lettering.

Meditate upon the Pentacle before closing your Personal Power Notebook with your right hand only. This, too, will "make it your own." Through mediation you will imbue it with your own psychic energy and charge it with your living Force.

Once you have done either of the above you are ready to consecrate your Pentacle. Here is Manning's chant for this consecration:

> Square of Power, Saturn's life,
>   Protect me ever more from strife.
> Bound to me by word and Light,
>   Keep me safe both day and night.
> A strong protector unto me,
>   And as my will, so mote it be!

Now your Power Medallion has one side—the Saturn side. The other side will look like this:

You now have two sides to one Medallion. Do this:

1. In your Personal Power Notebook, draw anew the Pentacles, one for Saturn, one for Jupiter (as in Figure 4).
2. Glue each to the two sides of one sheet of light cardboard (the side of a cereal box serves nicely).
3. Cut the cardboard to form the circle of your Medallion.

Now here is Manning's Secret revealed: the Saturn side of your Magic Medallion will protect you from harm, from accidents, from evil influences, from enemies, from negative forces and conditions. The Jupiter side will bring you wealth, riches, money, gold, pay raises—and all other forms of monetary gain.

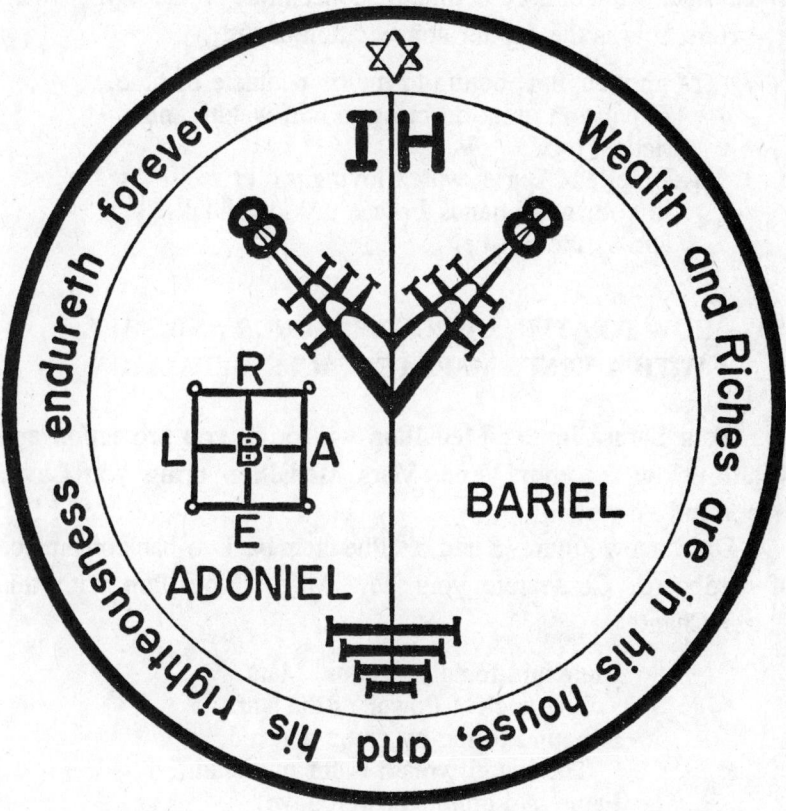

Figure 4: The Jupiter Pentacle

Remember: one side of your Medallion is called a Talisman. The two together, back to back, is a Magic Medallion. Wear it or carry it in purse or pocket. When you need protection, concentrate on one side; when in need of money, concentrate on the Jupiter side.

Here now is the Jupiter consecration chant:

> Mighty Jupiter, bound to me by pentacle of blue,
> Expansion great do bring to me, wealth and
> riches, too.
> Adoniel and Bariel watch lovingly o'er me.
> In your good hands I place my lot, thanks
> and so mote it be!

HOW TO ATTRACT POWER, HONOR AND LOVE WITH A VENUS-MARS PENTACLE MEDALLION

Your Saturn/Jupiter Medallion will bring you protection and wealth. Now let your Venus/Mars Medallion bring you Love, Honor and Power!

Draw anew Figures 5 and 6. Glue them back-to-back on a piece of cardboard. Consecrate your new Magic Medallion with this Power Chant:

> Male and female, Venus, Mars,
> The ancient Power of the stars,
> Is bound to me by green and red,
> The laurel wreath is for my head.
> Fame and honor, power, love,
> Rain down upon me from above.
> Mars and Venus bound to me,
> And as my will, so mote it be!

When Sheri Y. consecrated her Venus/Mars Medallion, she received a phone call that same evening. It was a gentleman she had been hoping to meet for more than a month. He asked for a date to take her to a very exclusive party—two dreams came true with one happy phone call! And the Power of the Medallion has lasted through courtship and a happy marriage.

Figure 5: The Venus Pentacle

You will be pleasantly amazed to see what your Magic Medallion will do in your life!

POWER-POINTERS

Remember: Everything you get in life, you obtain with the help
of unseen Forces.

The way to channel these Forces is to learn about mystic and
occult amulets, charms, pentacles and Medallions.

Choose your Stone by your birthdate and make your Amulet.

Study the Figures in this chapter and cut them out or copy them
to make your Magic Medallions.

Sit back and let Mystic and Occult Powers work in your life,
too!

Editor's Note on Power #9

This is a good place to make an additional note of importance
to you. It will be to your benefit to once in a while remember that
the Powers being provided for you throughout these dynamic pages
are offered by people just like yourself. Each and every Power has
been tried and tested by the Mystic Master who authored it. Remember: what the occultist has done, you can do!

To make the most of your Power #9, make a list for yourself.
Better yet, make *three* lists: one consisting of the people and influences from which you need protection; another of dreams and goals
you would like to see come true; and the third of *things* you would
like to own. Then tick them off with a check mark as your Amulet,
Pentacles and Medallions go to work!

In the next chapter you will achieve the Power to tap the
Occult World. The amazing key to this Power is provided
by occult Master Norvell. Here is the secret to opening a
whole new world for yourself!

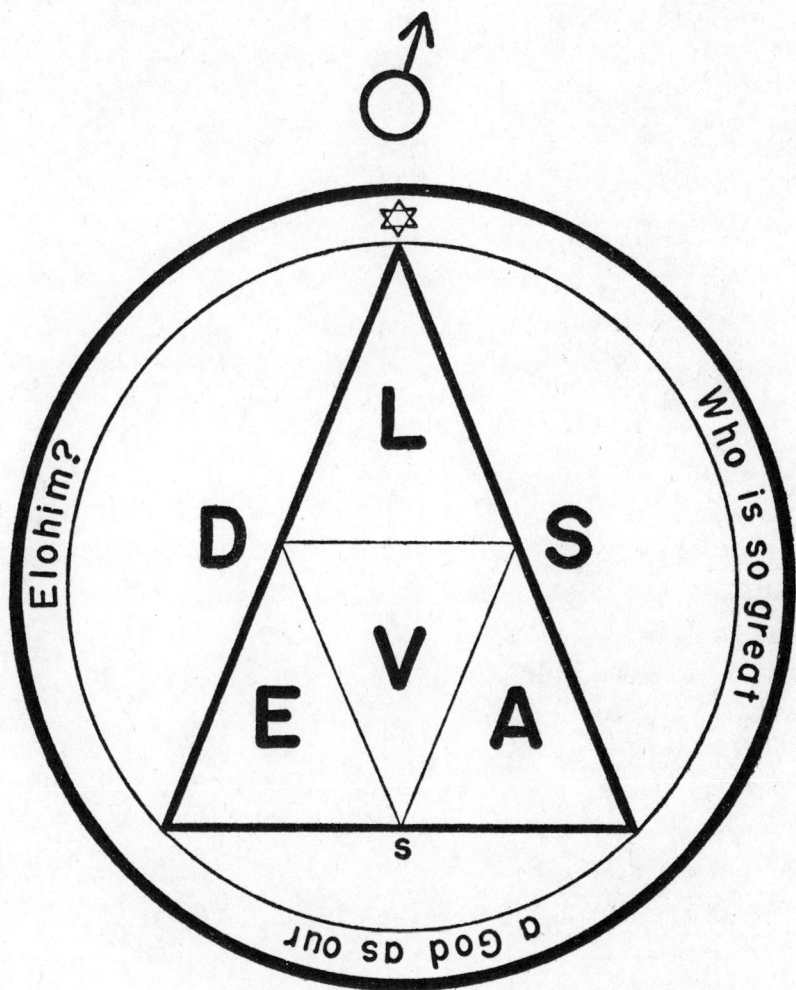

Figure 6: The Mars Pentacle

POWER 10

how to tap the power of the invisible world for a great new life

Riding the Cosmic Crest of Success

NORVELL'S REGIME FOR RELEASING
OCCULT POWER

I would like you to think of this chapter as your Reinforcement Power. It distills Norvell's Regime as set forth in his book *The Occult Sciences: How to Get What You Want Through Your Occult Powers*. The various occult and mystic Powers you have been learning step-by-step and page after page will bring you the beautiful and wonderful things you want out of life. As you know, practice is necessary. Study of each chapter is suggested. In addition to these, you need reinforcement of extrasensory abilities. This chapter will stimulate even further your latent occult and mystic Powers.

It has been my limited experience that every now and then there are those who encounter difficulty in reaping their share of occult and mystic benefits. Fortunately, we have the famous Norvell's regime for exciting and eliciting your dormant psychic Power.

If you have any difficulty in evoking your own occult and mystic abilities, follow these 8 easy steps:

1. To start the flow of occult Power through your higher brain centers it is important that you set aside a certain hour each day for your meditations and invocations. This can be in the morning when you start your day, or at night, before you retire.

Prepare a corner of your room with a small shrine, in which you have a white candle, some incense and a sacred relic in which you believe; this can be a religious emblem, a crucifix, or some other relic. You may have soft music playing in the background—something soothing and peaceful.

2. Sit in a comfortable position before your shrine, and prepare your mind and body for the visitation of higher occult forces by repeating the following occult creed. You may say this to yourself or aloud, or you may simply read it, until you have memorized it.

"I now dedicate myself to the occult principles of truth, beauty, good and intelligence that exist in the higher realms of the universe.

"I tap the occult force of cosmic power and I am now all powerful.

"I invoke the occult force of cosmic energy and the cells of my brain and body are now charged with dynamic life force and energy.

"I express life in every cell of my brain and body, and I now become vibrantly alive, healthy, strong, dynamically youthful and powerful.

"I now invoke the higher forces of the universe and I am in attunement with the creative principle that produces all riches and abundance."

3. When you have finished saying the above invocations, sit for a few moments in silent meditation. Mentally see the golden light of the sun flowing earthward, bathing your mind, body and soul with cosmic power. Now breathe deeply ten times and exhale slowly, as you visualize yourself standing in the center of a dynamic vortex of golden light. See this light flowing through every cell of your brain and body, and repeat the following invocation: I now absorb the golden light of occult power in every cell of my brain and body. I become the center of a vast constellation of occult Powers, which now express through my higher mind centers, giving me Power to be in tune with the infinite, knowing all secrets, and to be all-powerful and capable of performing miracles.

4. Now light the white candle and sit before it for a few moments in absolute silence. Let your mind now be receptive to the higher psychic pulsations that issue from the cosmic mind. As you make your mind a blank, pictures and thoughts may begin to flow into your mind centers. These can be psychic in nature, giving you valuable information that you can use. You can tune in on the higher thought forces of other minds while you are in such a state of deep meditation and know secrets that can benefit you.

5. While sitting in the silence ask for definite instructions or guidance. You can take with you in your meditations written requests on which you wish advice and guidance. These can be such questions as: How can I solve my problem? Where should I look for a better job? How can I get $1,000 that I need to pay my bills? Is this person suited to me for future marriage? Should I live in the city or the country?

How Gordon Was Psychically Helped to Attract the Sum of $20,000 Through Occult Power

Gordon W. was a student of occultism for only six months when he decided to sit in meditation and ask for a seemingly impossible sum of money. He wrote down the sum of $20,000 on a piece of paper and took it into his daily occult reverie. He asked the higher psychic centers of his mind to reveal how he could get this sum without delay, as he needed it to buy a new home for his family.

Gordon W. worked for a big advertising firm in New York City and was on a fixed salary. There didn't seem to be any chance to get that money right away, but he confidently asked his higher psychic centers to help him, and waited patiently to be shown the way.

One night Gordon W. had a dream in which he saw a product being advertised on television—one which his advertising firm handled. He saw the advertising campaign for that product, and it seemed to sell into the millions. He awakened from his psychic dream and wrote down his idea and then went to sleep.

The next day he approached the head of his firm with his idea for a new advertising campaign for their client's product. The manager liked the idea and put it entirely into Gordon W.'s hands. When the idea was put into a short movie, it was so sensational and the client was so pleased that he renewed a multi-million-dollar contract with the advertising firm.

The owners of the advertising firm were so delighted with the renewal of the contract that they advanced Gordon W. to an executive position and gave him a ten-thousand-dollar bonus!

Now Gordon W. was confident he would soon have his second ten thousand dollars. He went into occult reverie several times, and just like a dream, he saw a film unwinding giving him a new advertising campaign for a big cigarette company. This idea was put into action by his advertising firm and for this new commercial on television Gordon W. received another ten-thousand-dollar bonus, thus making the complete twenty thousand dollars for which he had asked.

6. There are several chords of occult rhythm to which you must be attuned. On your first day in meditation attune your mind to the occult chord of infinite intelligence. All knowledge may be known to you when you tap the higher occult forces that exist in cosmic mind. This infinite intelligence can be yours, by simply attuning yourself to knowledge and wisdom. Study and read each and every chapter in your Parker Lifetime Treasury of Mystic and Occult Powers. Prepare the centers of your mind for the reception of higher wisdom. As you sit in the silence, feel that you are contacting the infinite intelligence for every department of your life. Send out a mental golden line of infinite and contact the cosmic mind or God Power. Then sit quietly and wait for the reception of new and creative ideas from this infinite mind.

How a College Student Used the Occult Force of Infinite Intelligence to Make Superior Grades

Jimmy E. was a premed student whose father was a famous physician and surgeon, and Jimmy E. was expected to become a doctor. However, he was not a good student and in his premed work he had such low marks that there was grave danger he would never qualify for his medical course. He wanted to make his father proud of him, however, so he sought out the famous occultist, Norvell (your personal tutor in this chapter!), to ask for guidance as to his future.

Jimmy E. worked very hard to absorb the occult knowledge, but it was not easy, for he was not a natural student. Norvell gave him a regime to use at night while he slept, in which he would enlist the aid of higher occult Masters on the other planes of consciousness. After two weeks he reported that he was making progress in his studies. Some new mental higher centers seemed to open under the stimulus of his occult studies and he began to make better grades.

When it came time for his examinations before school closed for summer vacation, Jimmy E. completely depended on the occult Power of infinite intelligence. As a result he was perfectly relaxed and confident during his examination.

When the results were posted, Jimmy E. was surprised and delighted to find that he passed the examinations with the highest grades of anyone in his class! He went on to his medical studies that fall with a new determination, and graduated with high marks, becoming one of our finest specialists in New York City.

7. On the next day of meditation, attune your mind to the occult chord of infinite good. There is a vast reservoir of treasures in the invisible interstices of the universe; all our good comes from the cosmic spirit or intelligence. Each day when you start your activities give your higher mind centers this positive invocation for contacting the forces of good;

"I am now the center of my cosmic good. Every department of my life is blessed with that which is for my ultimate good. I attract good. I am good and I radiate goodness to everyone I meet."

8. On the next day of meditation, attune yourself to the occult chord of infinite love. Feel the divine emotion of love; radiate this emotion all day long to every person you meet. There is personal love and impersonal love. You must attune this occult chord daily, just as a violinist tunes his violin before he can have sweet music.

Say the following invocation for this tuning process to the chord of infinite love:

"I am now filled with the dynamic power of divine love. I am the center of universal love and I radiate love in my voice, my personality, my actions and my thoughts all day. I now magnetize others with this cosmic power of love and they are attracted to me for mutual good."

How Fern N. Saved Her Threatened Marriage with the Occult Chord of Love

Fern N. was a forty-five-year-old married woman with two children, who had come to my lecture work in New York City and learned about these occult forces that work in our lives. She had a very real problem. Her husband, who was fifty years old, had become interested in a younger woman who worked in his office and he wanted a divorce so he could marry this woman.

Fern N. began to use her occult powers to change this unfortunate situation. She asked for divine guidance in her daily meditation sessions. One day, while doing her housework, the answer came through quite clearly. Something told her psychically: You must work to win your husband's love once again. Give more time and attention to him and his needs. Be loving and forgiving and he will change for he still has love in his heart for you and your children.

Fern N. went on with her program of sending out love and forgiveness to her husband. She never discussed the other woman. She did not blame her husband nor nag him about his actions. She kept up this occult regime of sending out love and at night she "talked" to her husband silently before going to sleep, telling him how she loved him and that for the sake of their children, they should not divorce.

Within three weeks time her husband came to her and told her that he had changed his mind, that he did not want a divorce, and that he still loved Fern N. and wanted to keep the home intact. They had a complete reconciliation and went on to build a more solid and enduring marriage than they had known before.

QUESTIONS AND ANSWERS ABOUT
OCCULT POWER

Question: Can I expect such miracles in my life, too?
Answer: Study diligently and you will learn to tap the *higher occult forces* that geniuses have used throughout history to achieve their extraordinary miracle Powers.

Question: What I want to know is: Will occult Power help me to pick the winner of tomorrow's race?
Answer: Yes, occult Power can do even that! Through this study you are undertaking your occult Power will unleash unlimited dimensions of mind and spirit, which can cause you to know the future in advance, no matter *why* you want to know it.

Question: I'm only eighteen; how can I use occult Power?
Answer: Do you wish to become rich? Do you want to attract people who can help you achieve your life goal? Are you interested in becoming more magnetic, dynamic and attractive? You will learn how to tap the *psycho-magnetic wavelengths* in the cosmos and channel them to your higher mind centers to work living miracles.

THE POSITIVE SPECTRUM OF
OCCULT POWER

Occultism deals with the positive spectrum of cosmic power. You must know what these positive occult forces are; then you can easily release their potent Power in your daily life and achieve health, happiness, prosperity, peace of mind, romantic fulfillment, and spiritual completion.

MASTER MYSTIC KEY

The Two Polarities of Occult Power

Positive and Constructive	*Negative and Destructive*
Intelligence	Ignorance
Good	Evil
Love	Hate
Happiness	Misery

Positive and Constructive	Negative and Destructive
Beauty	Ugliness
Health	Sickness
Life	Death
Riches	Poverty
Peace	War
Charity	Miserliness
Heaven	Hell
God	Devil

Now make your own list of such polarities, drawing them from your own personal life. Then accentuate the positive and eliminate the negative!

OCCULTOMATIC POWER STIMULATOR

Dedicate yourself as a positive channel for the projection of creative occult Power.

Withdraw into a quiet room where you may be alone for your daily occult work. Have a white candle burning. Visualize the occult force flowing from the infinite, like the golden rays of the sun that bathe the earth. See these powerful rays penetrating your mind, body and soul, as the focal point of your own personal Power.

Repeat to yourself the following invocation, as you focus this creative occult ray in your consciousness:

> I am the center of life, light, and intelligence. I now relax my mind and body, and let the divine flood of life-giving energy, Power, and glory to flow in and through my mind, body, and soul. I am vibrantly alive. I am filled with the life force and cosmic rhythm of health, youth, vitality, and joy. All I wish is mine!

POWER-POINTERS

Use your new occult Power to:

1. Place yourself in a divine state of occult reverie.

2. Obtain information regarding the events of your life—past, present or future.

3. Bid your subconscious to work miracles in your life.

4. Activate fourth-dimensional Power in your daily life to make you healthy, wealthy, and wise.

5. Contact the minds of other people to know their thoughts, ideas, and intentions. Forewarned is forearmed!

6. Change a dissatisfying existence into life more abundant!

Editor's Note on Power #10

Study this chapter as diligently and carefully as you have studied the preceding nine and you will reinforce your own occult Power.

Make a comprehensive list of the things you want in your life here and now. Date this list. Then practice Norvell's regime and watch the results. Check off each goal and dream as it is manifested in reality for you. And enjoy!

When you become attuned to the cosmic wavelength of peace and joy through these occult rituals and invocations, practices and studies, your life will take on new depth and you will truly find the Power for which your soul has yearned since the beginning of time.

Make this and all the others—*Your Power!*

As if you did not now possess enough Power to alter the very world—there follows yet another! The Parker family of occultists and mystics wants every area of your life to be renewed, empowered, full of happiness. Your next Power is control over the emotions and love of the opposite sex! How would you like to COMMAND love? Read on!

POWER 11

how to magnetize, attract and command love

How Mind Cosmology Can Magnetize, Attract, and Hold Your Desired Mate

You were created to know and experience true love. For every person there is a true soul mate. When you once learn how to use the laws of Mind Cosmology, you can magnetize and attract your true soul mate in love and marriage. No matter what your age, love is the indispensable element that can make your life complete.

As Browning said, "Take away love and the earth is a tomb."

You will have love—rich, fulfilling, exciting, pleasurable, exalting LOVE.

In this chapter you will learn how to use Love Power, for it reveals the secret doctrine of cosmic energy and teaches you how to translate your inner dreams of love into the outer reality you desire! The Master Key to this secret—once again—is provided by that famous mystic, Norvell in his book *Mind Cosmology*. In these pages he reveals the smooth occult pathway to true love.

You will learn how to magnetize and attract into the orbit of your life experience the mate who will respond to your love magnetically and emotionally and be the perfect mate for you.

All you have to do is absorb the meaning of Mind Cosmology—and then let the occult force work for you.

QUESTIONS AND ANSWERS ABOUT MIND
COSMOLOGY—THE LOVE COMMAND POWER

Question: Can you explain Mind Cosmology to me?
Answer: Mind Cosmology is the new science of the space age. It deals with the miraculous forces that exist in the invisible cosmos, which man may tap with his mind and channel to his everyday life for every constructive purpose. This science is as old as time and space and yet as new as tomorrow's newest scientific revelations.

Question: How does Mind Cosmology fit in with my new occult Powers?
Answer: Through Mind Cosmology you may cross the invisible, mystic threshold of consciousness and enter into another dimension of mind Power. Through this mystical extension of the human mind and spirit you can channel the miracle-working Power of a cosmic mind that operates in all nature.

Question: I am seventy-one years old and the person I love is almost ten years younger. Can I still know the joy of union?
Answer: Age and time is no barrier. The cosmic mind that created the universe is a Power that is available to you. You may tap this Power and use it to achieve the great love you desire.

HOW MRS. RITA L. USED MIND COSMOLOGY
TO RENEW HER LOVE LIFE

A woman attended one of Norvell's lectures and told him she had continual fatigue, headaches, and general feeling of debility. She said, "I feel that something awful is going to happen and I am powerless to stop it."

Norvell then learned that she was married and had two children, but had separated from her husband because he had been going around with another woman.

Rita L. still loved her husband, and she was now living without

love and an outlet for her deep emotions. The husband came to see
the children frequently and there had been no talk of a divorce.

Norvell told Rita L. that she must make an attempt to heal the
broken marriage, but she complained, "How can I take him back
when I know he's been with another woman?"

Then Norvell gave Rita the Mind Cosmology regime for winning and holding true love, which would guarantee that her husband, when he once returned to her, would never leave her for
another woman.

Rita began working on this program of Mind Cosmology. She
took her husband back after he told her he did not love the other
woman but that it was only a temporary affair. She began to build
the new self-image of love and romance in her home, and soon she
and her husband were in a more loving and harmonious relationship
than they had been in all the five years of previous marriage. Now,
three years later, Norvell still hears from Rita L., and love has
lasted, bringing her every joy she had expected from life.

The miracle Rita L. enjoyed, you, too, can enjoy! Here is
Norvell's regime, which he gave to Rita, and now shares with you:

MASTER MYSTIC KEY

This regime includes five points:

1. *To forgive her husband and take him back for the sake of
   their children, and to never mention again her jealousy or
   suspicion, but act as though she trusted him implicitly.*

2. *She was to completely restyle her self-image from an ordinary housewife into one of glamour, beauty and magnetism,
   through a regime which I gave her, and which we shall
   discuss later in this chapter.*

3. *She was to practice the art of expressing love not only in a
   physical relationship, but on a mental and spiritual plane as
   well. She was to see her husband as her true soul mate, the
   father of her two wonderful children and as the man God
   intended to be her mate for life.*

4. *She was to mentally weave a spell of romance and beauty over her husband's mind, by creating the atmosphere for perpetual love in her mind, and in her home. She was to prepare herself for his arrival each night from work, and be ready to join him in his various experiences and needs, and not be so exhausted from housework that her husband became a secondary interest in her life.*

5. *She was to break the negative mesmerism of the drudgery of her daily life by going out more often, finding ways to leave the children with a responsible person, while she danced, went to movies, or shared in bowling or other activities that could bring her and her husband into a closer partnership and friendship.*

HOW YOU CAN TAP THE POWER OF MIND COSMOLOGY TO ENHANCE YOUR LOVE LIFE

Love is your passport to unlimited happiness. But this passport is not issued by the government. You obtain it from within, where Christ said the Kingdom of God lay. That Kingdom is Powerful— what sceptics call "occult," as if it were "forbidden." Christ asked no government for permission to use his Power of Love. Nor will you! You will tap your own hidden reservoir of this Power as you study and assimilate Norvell's teachings about Mind Cosmology.

Get comfortable. Relax. And digest the following remarkable regime designed to bring you Love, lOve, loVe, lovE!

OCCULTOMATIC POWER STIMULATOR

1. Attune your mind to the glorious harmony of love. Just as a musician must tune his violin to make sweet music, so too your mind and heart and soul must be daily attuned to the divine chord of love.

Each day, when you start your day, give yourself a magnetic suggestion: "All day I shall be attuned to the high vibrations of love. My thoughts, words, and acts shall be loving. I shall do nothing today that reflects jealousy, suspicion, animosity or hate. I am charged with the vibrations of God's divine romance and I shall so conduct myself all day."

2. Magnetize your mind centers with the vibrations of spiritual love by reading beautiful love poetry and reciting poems, until you have captured the beauty and spirit of spiritual love. The poems of Elizabeth Barrett Browning are specially suited to this purpose. The poem, "How do I Love Thee?" should be memorized by every person who wishes to capture the spirit of love forevermore in his heart.

The magnificent poetry of Shakespeare in his *Venus and Adonis*, is also to be read and enthroned in consciousness. Poetry often reflects more than anything else the cosmic spirit of divine love.

3. Practice each day releasing the emotion of love on all planes of consciousness. Love is more than a physical attraction between two people; it is a mental and spiritual expression as well. Learn to attune your mind to that of the beloved, hold similar interests, study things together, plan events that you may share, so you build a unity of interests that binds you together on more than one plane of expression. Most young people make the mistake of falling in love with the physical person, and they fail to see the spiritual person behind the material facade of life.

4. The law of romantic attraction in Mind Cosmology decrees that like attracts like. You can only attract the true soul mate when you both vibrate on the same plane of consciousness.

Mentally select the mental and spiritual qualities you desire in a mate. Write these down on a romantic chart. Put down a physical description of the mate first; then make out a list of the mental qualities you desire. Your list, if you are a man, might look like this:

I desire a woman who is of medium height, slender, with grace and charm. Blonde hair, blue eyes; even, regular features. I want the following qualities in my future wife:

She is to be kind and gentle, having consideration for others.

She should be unselfish and desire a loving husband, a good home, and a family of two or three children.

I want a wife who will be a good hostess in the home; one who will be interested in music, art and good books. A woman who enjoys athletic events and can share with me my interest in all sports.

I want a wife with a good home background, from a family where there was love and unity, and a spiritual background and good, sound moral values.

5. If a woman, you can make out the romantic chart with the specifications you desire in a future soul mate. The reason you must know what these qualities are, is that you cannot attract such a person unless you vibrate to the same level of mental and spiritual inspiration.

6. Do not merely look at the physical being, but check on character, qualities of honesty and integrity; a mate who is concerned about other people; one who believes in God and is of the same religious faith as yourself.

7. There are eight stages of romantic ecstasy which can be built between any loving couple. When these are established in the relationship, nothing can shatter such a union:

A. You will enjoy doing the same things; you will have the same interest in hobbies, sports, social activities and you will enjoy the same type of books, music and art.

B. You will both operate on the same plane of high moral standards of honesty, goodness, truth, charity and idealism.

C. You will both be repelled by vulgarity, lying, cheating, stealing, immoral conduct, and infractions of the Ten Commandments. You will share a desire to idealize yourselves and build perfection in mind and body.

D. You will have so much magnetism between each other that you will want to be together constantly sharing the same emotions, friends, experiences and entertainments.

E. You will respond emotionally to the same high standards of beauty in art, music, literature. You will share the enjoyment of the wonders of nature, building similar interests in sports and outdoor activities that are healthful and enjoyable.

F. You will magnetize and attract a circle of friends who have your interests, similar personalities, and basically enjoy the same type of humor and conversation.

G. In this romantic relationship you will have an unselfish desire to share all your wonderful experiences with your beloved. This includes all your good fortune, your money, your secrets, your ideas and ideals, never excluding your mate from the bonds of intimacy and personal relationship.

H. You will create strong bonds of physical and sexual love, that will outlast the first magnetic attraction which might have been physical. You will add, as you grow older, the spiritual type of love that will encompass not only your family but God and the world.

8. Learn to weave a spell of romantic entrancement about the mind and heart of the beloved. This is done by mentally projecting the thoughts of love, beauty and goodness that you want to lodge in the mind and soul of the soul mate. Each night, when you go to sleep, look at a photograph of the person you want to marry; or if you do not have a photograph, hold the person's face in the forefront of your mind. Then talk to that astral image; weave your romantic spell of entrancement with the following words:

I project my loving thoughts to you before going to sleep. I love you and I believe you are my true soul mate. If it is God's will, we shall be together for an eternity. I want to share with you every beautiful and loving experience I have in my future. I ask that you respond to my love with the same emotion and intensity I now feel. I caress you, and in my heart and soul, I know that God intended for us to marry and have a beautiful family. You will sense this magnetic projection and will respond with love.

HOW TO CONSTRUCT THE PROPER ASTRAL IMAGE OF YOUR HEART'S DESIRE

Vagueness is the worst enemy of occult Power. While occult Power certainly works from your subconscious mind, it is of vital importance that you send to it a proper image of your heart's desire. Let's say, for example, that you are lonely, that you want a mate, that you have no clear cut picture of what you want, that no certain person comes to mind. How then do you avail yourself of fulfilling love? Very simply, you *put in your order* for what you want!

Answer the following questions yourself, writing in your Personal Power Notebook only. When the questionnaire is completed, project the resulting image to your subconscious mind and permit Mind Cosmology to do the rest.

1. How tall should my soul mate be?
1. ....

2. How much should my soul mate weigh?
2. ....

3. What color hair?
3. ....

4. Eyes?
4. ....

5. What sort of personality should my soul mate have?
5. Check one: ( ) sunny· ( ) happy; ( ) sedate; ( ) serious; ( ) gay; ( ) sparkling.

6. What outdoor activities should my soul mate enjoy?
6. ....

7. What indoor activities should my soul mate enjoy?
7. ....

8. What common interests should we have?
8. ....

9. How do I want to be treated?
9. ....

YOUR PERSONAL MYSTIC METER FOR
MEASURING YOUR LOVE POWER

Love Power is potent! It is a force coming through you to change not only your life but the lives of people around you. "Love for All" is an ancient mystic axiom. By all means, study this chapter carefully and take notes, but do not forget others. The more love you send to others, the more you get for yourself. Find the answer to each question below which in any way applies to you. WRITE DOWN YOUR ANSWERS. Then meditate upon them as these chapters have taught you. Emit love, transmit love, emanate love. This section will help you to reap a harvest of love for yourself as well as help you to share that limitless love with your fellow man.

Love in My Personal Life

What would be the ideal use of Love Power in my life?

What can I do today to create an atmosphere of love?

What part of my physical body does my subconscious mind tell me to work on?

What can I do today to attract and please my mate?

Love on the Job

Am I using my occult Love Power in my work?

How can I show love toward a fellow employee? The boss? A subordinate?

Which person around me obviously *needs* love?

What loving thing can I do to make others like me?

Love in My Future

What am I doing today to insure love tomorrow?

Am I using my imaging Power to create long-lasting love for me and mine?

What can I do mentally and invisibly to perpetuate friendship?

How can I use my occult and mystic Powers to help others find love?

POWER-POINTERS

You were created to know and experience love. If love has passed you by or is strained in your life, practice Norvell's Power technique to get Love flowing again throughout your life.

For every person there is a true soul mate. Loneliness need not be your lot in life. Study this chapter slowly. Write down important personal keys that "ring a bell" with you. Get in touch with your subconscious mind through the outlined instructions. Get Love!

Study the 8-point Occultomatic Power Stimulator until love is flooding every area of your existence.

Editor's Note on Power #11

Watch for ways in which you have already been using Love Power—without knowing it! Write down those ways, now that you know what Love Power is in your Personal Power Notebook.

Take each point in Norvell's 8-point Occultomatic Power Stimulator—one a day (like a vitamin)—and learn it by heart. Attune your mind to the very source of occult and mystic Power.

Record any and all phrases, sentences, keys, tips, or paragraphs that strike you as essential knowledge for your betterment.

Do not feel limited to these suggestions. Make as many notes as you wish, keying your notes to your Personal Power Notebook. You may want to photocopy some pages and paste them right in your Notebook.

Treasure your book, treasure your chapters, and treasure your Powers, but, by all means, also treasure your own ideas, intuitions and insights placed in your Personal Power Notebook as these Power-packed pages evoke them for you. They are often the most secret aspects of personal Power.

The next Power on your agenda is provided by occult Master Al G. Manning. Much has been said pro and con about Astral Projection. Al Manning expertly rips away the shrouds of mystery and makes available to you this amazing Power to fulfill your Will, your Wishes, and your Wants. Manning will show you how—without hocus-pocus—to work your will on the invisible planes of existence.

how to use the power of astral travel for a bright new future

How to Awaken Your Latent Ability to
Astral Travel for Profit and Success

We will not waste time and space trying to convince the skeptic that it is possible to separate the consciousness from the body and travel apart from it. If everyone else in the world is doing it, but *you* can't, it doesn't exist for you. Conversely, if no one else can do it, but *you* can, then it is real to you and you will take care not to be talked out of it.

Our approach will be to give you a choice of several techniques—each developed by occult Master Manning—with the suggestion that you give *each* method a good try. "Just *one* experience of full separation," says this noted psychic investigator, "will explain more to you than a whole book full of words and pictures."

Aside from the material benefits enjoyed by many astral travelers, there is this common report: You *know* you will live after your body has been buried in the ground! This assurance alone is well worth the faith required to experience astral travel. But your Treasury of occult and mystic Powers does not stop there. If you are going to astral travel, you are going to do so in order to better your life here and now, grow rich, happier, more successful.

I want you to ask yourself some reasonable questions right now. The answers you supply are for yourself alone. Just ask yourself:

If I could combat the vicious attacks of an enemy *without lifting a finger*, would I do it?

If there were a way to make a distant loved one (even a *departed* loved one) as close to me as if he or she were actually physically present, would I do it?

If I could influence my boss to give me a pay raise in a non-physical manner, would I employ the method?

If I could attract money to me magically, would I use the magic?

If you have answered "Yes" to any of the above questions, astral travel is for you!

So let's get to it! In what follows, Al G. Manning in his *The Miracle of Universal Psychic Power* provides you with all you need know to benefit wonderfully and surprisingly from this amazing Power. Follow the instructions carefully (write some of them out to impress them upon your mind) and you will reap the same harvest of profit and success that many of Manning's students have.

HOW TO PROGRAM YOUR SUBCONSCIOUS TO WAKE YOU ON THE ASTRAL

The simplest way to perform an astral projection is to just wake up from a nap or a night's sleep with the two bodies still separated. We will discuss ways to tell the difference between a valid projection and a dream, but let's get to the technique first so that we will have some inputs to evaluate.

MASTER MYSTIC KEY

Instructions:

1. Take a piece of scotch tape and a small object without sharp edges (your Lucky Stone will do) to your meditation place (favorite chair, bedroom, etc.).

2. *In lieu of an actual meditation stone, a paper clip will do.*
   Have a mirror handy, either on a wall or in your hand.

3. *Attach the paper clip (or whatever you are using) to the*
   mirror with the scotch tape.

4. *Address the mirror in this fashion: "This paper clip will be*
   your reminder to wake me up after the separation of the
   astral and the physical bodies has been effected. You are to
   return me to full waking consciousness in the astral body
   that we may continue to become more effective through this
   new understanding. You may awaken my physical body
   after I return to it, then I will remove the paper clip and
   make notes on the experience."

5 *Then go to bed and drift off to a normal sleep in a mood of*
   happy expectancy.

6. *Try this Manning Method a few times. Once you have ex-*
   perienced astral projection it will become second nature to
   vou— and you will be able to do anything with it!

QUESTIONS AND ANSWERS CONCERNING
YOUR POWER TO PROJECT
YOURSELF ASTRALLY

Question: I know I mustn't be discouraged if it doesn't work the
first time, but what if it doesn't work the second or third time?
Answer: Even if you don't have 100 percent success at first, you
are very apt to remember some part of your evening's experience.
Be sure to compliment your reflection in the mirror for any tiny
experience and tell it that it is on the right track. The compliments
and praise will help your subconscious to develop the ability to
bring you to full astral consciousness over a period of time.

Question: How can you tell the difference between a dream and an
astral projection?
Answer: As a rule of thumb, remember this: Dreams may be in
black and white or in very subdued colors, but an astral experience
is characterized by the special vividness of the colors. Once you

have seen astral colors, you will know what I mean. Astral colors often mix without blending; for instance, an object can appear equally red and blue at the same time without any sensation of purple.

Question: How can I know definitely that I am astrally traveling?
Answer: Do not be dependent upon objective verification. Remember that faith plays a very large part in this highly subjective experience. If you are not sure about a particular experience, temporarily accept it as astral so that you can compliment your subconscious and encourage it to bring more definite experiences.

HOW TO PREPARE YOURSELF FOR
ASTRAL TRAVEL

Presumably you wish to travel astrally *for a reason*. Have this reason clear in your mind. It is wise to first make a short list of exactly what you expect to gain from your new Power. Do you want wealth? Health? Friendship? Control over negative elements? Power over enemies? More fun out of life? A lover? A marriage partner? Communication with the departed? With the distant and absent?

Get clear about what you want and have this wish, goal or dream implanted firmly in your mind before you begin your astral exercise. You can travel astrally to any place in the outer and inner universes, so think big and think strongly. Desire with gusto and verve!

HOW A DEPARTED MOTHER SAVED HER
LOVED ONES FROM POVERTY

D.J. had this experience to report: "I had practiced the subconscious programming to wake up on the astral about a week; then my mother died. My work was then interrupted by a trip home to help my father get things in order and arrange the funeral. The night after the funeral, I remembered my astral practice and decided to try, even though I was away from my normal meditation place.

"I used the vanity table in the extra bedroom and taped my meditation stone to the mirror, with the usual instructions to my mirrored reflection. When I dozed off to sleep, I suddenly realized that I was sitting in the living room with my mother. The colors were unbelievably vivid and I knew that this was the astral. Mother looked very good, but seemed interested only in showing me an envelope that was taped under the silverware drawer in the kitchen. It was a terribly short time and then she was gone. I didn't wait until morning, but woke up in my body and went straight to the drawer. There in an envelope were ten crisp $100 bills! Dad had been hard pressed by the funeral expenses, and that thousand dollars sure helped. Mom had saved it for an emergency and took my astral trip as a way to get us the message. Even better was the feeling for Dad and me that indeed Mom still lives and cares about us."

THE CONSCIOUSNESS COLLECTION
TECHNIQUE FOR CONSCIOUS PROJECTION

Recognition that you have been conscious on the astral will make the techniques of separating the two bodies while you are awake much easier. The technique provided now by Manning will more or less split the difference between waking on the astral and a projection from full waking consciousness.

Read the following instructions at least three times before acting upon them. Get familiar with the occult knowledge presented in your Treasury. The more familiar it is to you, the better your chances of exciting and amazing results.

OCCULTOMATIC POWER STIMULATOR

Preparation for astral travel requires only that you find a quiet place to lie down where your body will not be disturbed. Lie comfortably on your back with your eyes closed and begin consciously to direct your breathing process. Use the lower back muscles for deep diaphragmatic breathing as slowly as you find comfortable.

Each time you inhale, mentally gather the individual consciousness from each cell of your body to a collection point at your brow center. It helps to divide the body into imaginary sections for this exercise. Begin by gathering the consciousness from your feet, next your lower legs, then the upper legs, etc.

When you feel that you have gathered a good measure of the body's total consciousness at the brow center, continue to visualize the remaining bits of consciousness coming from all over the body as you inhale; then as you exhale, begin to project this collected consciousness to a point of Light you imagine on the ceiling. As you continue collecting on the inhalation and projecting as you exhale, one of two things will happen. Either you will slip into a light sleep and enter a projection like those when your subconscious mind wakes you on the astral, or you will suddenly become aware that you are conscious on the ceiling, floating comfortably above your body.

The Time Element

How long should it take to get out? This is my favorite bed time technique; for me it never seems to take more than ten to 15 breaths before my astral body is off somewhere. But the first few times you try you may be excessively nervous about it and temporarily block your projection. Spend no more than 20 minutes at a time on this in your beginning work. If that does not get you out of the body, tell yourself that you will work on relaxation and try again later. Most people can achieve projection on at least one of the first three tries, but it may take those with a nervous nature longer. With this method, *practice will surely get you out* of the body, sooner or later.

Jerry Y. ran into the only pitfal in this method. He wrote to complain, "By the fourth breath I'm completely asleep. How do I get around that?"

This requires picking a definite target place to go in your astral body. Visualize your target place in three-dimensional living color and keep the image bright and clear as you perform your Occultomatic Power Stimulator.

You may argue later that you were "only dreaming," but there will be an experience *in the target place*. Jerry's report on the change was: "I fell asleep on the living room couch and picked the back bathroom as my target place. It was a most interesting experience. I remember breathing on the couch, then suddenly I was floating above the wash basin in the bathroom. I will never forget the vividness of the porcelain in the basin! I was there only a few seconds before I popped back into my physical body, but I understand and I'm getting the hang of it now."

HOW TO LET THE OCCULTOMATIC POWER STIMULATOR FLOAT YOU OUT OF YOUR BODY

A. *Prepare yourself for astral travel according to the instructions in your Occultomatic Power Stimulator.*

B. *Lie down, close your eyes, and imagine a great wheel of Light inside your head.*

C. *Now pretend that this wheel is ascending right through the top of your head.*

D. *Consider this wheel your personal flying saucer.*

E. *Deliberately climb aboard it in consciousness.*

F. *When you feel yourself near the ceiling, leave your astral body right there and descend your consciousness back down to your physical body.*

G. *Pass your consciousness between the two bodies three or four times.*

H. *Then take conscious control, and with the bright aura you built during the exercise you can enjoy a truly lovely astral experience.*

I. *When you want to come back to the physical body, all that is necessary is to gently will yourself to settle back into the same hole you went out in the top of your head.*

Manning's Note to the Fearful: You are in no danger of being "trapped" in the astral plane. If something should startle you, you

will pop right back into your physical body instantly. Fear defeats
the purpose of astral travel. Actually, once you get the hang of it,
you will be pleasantly surprised to discover that you have been
unconsciously traveling astrally for quite some time! Astral travel is
no more dangerous than self-hypnosis. And it can be just as beneficial, helpful, creative, positive, and fulfilling!

Some people get so excited wnen they learn to travel astrally
that they fail to use the Power constructively. This is understand-
able, but after the first few successes, you should begin using your
new Power as a potent tool for your own betterment and the betterment of others. This Power will greatly enhance every aspect of
your life—in business, domestic affairs, social activities . . . every
side of your life.

You will learn to use this Power any time and in any place,
even away from your meditation place. Some adepts travel astrally
at will—whenever they get the urge. Test your new Power for ten
days. Try using it to solve your problems. That's what it is for! See
how it immediately reduces your troubles to a minimum. See how it
launches you into a fuller, richer life, the kind of life you want and
deserve—starting right now!

Here is a small outline to get you started. Think of a problem,
any problem you now have, and consider in what ways astral travel
can help you personally to solve it. Write down the problem and
course of action in your Personal Power Notebook.

The Problem ....
Here is what I shall do on the astral plane:
1. ....
   ....
2. ....
   ....
3. ....
   ....
4. ....
   ....

So far you have been studying the Beginner's section of astral knowledge. Now let occultist Manning take you forward to the study for Advanced Students.

HOW TO ACHIEVE SPONTANEOUS ASTRAL POWER WHILE FULLY CONSCIOUS

As you work to seek projection of your "astral beingness," you are setting fresh psychic currents in motion. Thus you may be treated to a spontaneous or unplanned (by you) astral trip. Even if you have been unable to get out of your physical body by using the exercises, you may be treated to a projection because of your demonstrated interest and sincerity. These spontaneous projections generally involve an opportunity to be of service to another being.

Since this type of experience is spontaneous, I cannot tell you how to do it. But making yourself familiar with the possibility and with the whole idea of the astral you can make a pleasant and rewarding experience out of something that might otherwise cause quite a fright.

Additional Techniques for Fully Conscious Astral Power

The classic technique for conscious projection requires a touch of Yoga. The mind can assert control of the normally involuntary functions by concentration and practice. Here it is necessary to control the heartbeat and consequently the blood pressure. If you are a heart patient, I'd advise you to skip this section, but any normally healthy person can do it. Focus your attention on your physical heart and *feel* it beating. This is a natural process that may take from three seconds to three minutes to do well. Next, begin to count in time with your heartbeats: "One, two three, four . . ." When you reach ten, start over with one again. When you feel the counting and the heartbeat well synchronized, gradually slow down the counting and "will" the heart to do likewise. Just a little practice should bring the ability to slow the heart down by 20 to 30 percent, which is plenty for our purposes.

When you can control your heartbeat, you are ready to try the projection. Just follow these easy instructions:

Lay your body down in a safe, quiet place. Breathe very slowly and deeply as you slow your heartbeat more and more. Soon you will feel the physical body lessening its grip on the astral; then simply will yourself to float, or imagine that you are floating up out of your body. Some people experience a moment of dizziness or nausea as the bodies separate, but don't be alarmed. Just accept that as the indication that the technique is working, and float up until you are completely free. We will discuss what to do after you get out, but let's touch one more way of getting out first.

See the place you want to be and will your consciousness to travel there. Think of it as if you were diving into the water—just a happy astral jump. When G.N. was practicing this technique, his spirit guides often helped with an invitation to a semi-spontaneous projection. As he sat in meditation, they flashed a symbol of a golden ankh in front of him with the place he was invited to visit showing through the loop of the cross. With this came the urge to dive in. He explained it to me with the comment: "It is an utterly delicious feeling to dive through that ankh and feel the curving of my astral back as I arch my astral body to put me back into an upright position."

Practice is the secret of building the disciplines of certain success.

HOW TO CONTROL YOUR
ASTRAL PROJECTIONS

For most of us the first few astral projections seem not too well-controlled—you go or are somehow sent places seemingly capriciously, and the least bit of fright may send you back into your physical body with a nerve-shattering jerk. But it is certainly no worse a challenge than learning to walk is to a baby. We gain a reasonable amount of expertise by trial and error, but the fine points will require a degree of discipline. The vehicle of astral travel is most frequently called the astral body, but we can understand more of its nature by studying the other names for it. The astral is a realm of emotion and desire; thus various systems have called the astral body the *desire body*, or the *body of emotion*.

Reflection upon your "out-of-control" astral experiences will quickly show you that some strong (thought perhaps previously unconscious) emotion simply ignored the directions of your mind and carried you where it wanted to go. Thus we can quickly agree that control of your emotions will bring control of your astral experiences. But we must be careful here. We can never control our emotions by stifling them! This battle is won only on the positive thinking, metaphysical level. We appeal to the emotions on a positive note such as, "Oh, wouldn't it be nice to . . ."

Importance of Mood Factor

You will also recognize the necessity of being in a good mood when you attempt to leave the body. If you are full of anger and resentment, the power of these negative emotions will drag you off to some kind of nightmare experience or an astral confrontation where you are at a big disadvantage. Avoidance of the negative should be natural to you from our earlier work, but how shall we induce the positive and effective part?

Desire is the power of the astral; thus a planned set of desires will act like railroad tracks and guide you unerringly along your chosen path. While you are in your physical body is the time to decide where you want to go, and to develop the most positive selling presentation to your astral beingness. For instance, you may want to visit your mother who is in the spirit world. If you think of the misery of "losing her to the grim reaper" and build a negative, clinging desire, you will find yourself producing a nightmarish astral experience that will shoot you right back into your physical body. The same desire couched in the happy idea, "It would be so nice to drop in on mother for a friendly visit," will clear a path to that kind of happy visit.

Similarly, to the frequent question, "Why can't I get out on the astral to check up on my husband and see if he is really working late?'' there can be only one answer. ''Your jealousy and fear either lock you in your physical body or take you to the area of miserable thoughtforms and pop you right back. Try a constructive use of the faculty and it will work for you.''

PRACTICAL AND SPIRITUAL APPLICATIONS OF YOUR ASTRAL POWER

The friendly visit with a loved one in spirit, or a quick trip to a relative's house so you can call her in the morning and compliment her on the new furniture arrangement, may be pleasant and fun, but there are many more practical uses of the Power to travel on the astral. There are two major uses of intense practical value: first, getting help in solving pressing problems of this life; second, and perhaps more important, getting guidance and spiritual instruction—literally recovering the time previously lost in sleep for cultural, educational, and spiritual pursuits.

Practical problem-solving can come on the level of your need.

When there are no major problems requiring attention, accept it as a time for the spiritual seeking that will insure a better future. Plan a projection to your spirit guides with the idea of asking for instruction in those subjects that *they* consider important to you.

As you can see your astral Power may be used for spiritual as well as material needs. More money, better luck, greater love, happier friendships, pay raises, promotions, less enmity and adversity, spiritual awakening, mystic knowledge, occult forces—all this and more is waiting for you as you apply your astral Power on a solid basis that balances the practical world with spiritual seeking.

POWER-POINTERS

1. The only meaningful proof of astral projection comes from *your* personal experience of separation from your body.

2. Use the technique of programming your consciousness to wake you up on the astral as an easy way to get acquainted with the

work. The familiarity you gain in this manner will make deliberate conscious separation from the body much easier.

3. The best way to distinguish an astral trip from a dream is by the extreme vividness of the astral colors.

4. The technique of collecting the consciousness by deep diaphragmatic breathing and projecting it through the brow center is a very popular method. It may bring about a full conscious separation or take you through a momentary sleep to consciousness on the astral.

5. Other methods of conscious separation from the physical body include floating out the top of your head during the psychic development exercise, projection through the astral speaking tube, or conscious control of the heartbeat to slow it down and reduce the body's grip on you. Try them all to see which works best for you.

6. Prepare yourself psychologically to accept the spontaneous projections. Your spirit people may borrow you to help another being in need or to bring a special experience of value to you—if you are relaxed enough to accept and *let it happen*.

7. Control of where you go on the astral comes from learning the positive control of your emotions. A light and happy attitude gives the maximum of control.

8. The possibilities of practical application of astral projection are infinite. Use it for problem-solving of all kinds, and for gaining the spiritual instruction that leads to major jumps in your material progress.

Editor's Note on Power #12

Make a list of goals, dreams and wishes that you would like to see come true. Formulate one at a time in your mind so that it is clear, concise and direct. As you solve each problem or attain each desire through astral Power, check that one off the list with a definite black checkmark. Cancel it in your mind so it does not recur.

Look around you. Are there others in need? Use your astral Power to help them. Visit the sick, the imprisoned, and "work" on their astral spirits to help them get well. *You* will reap a harvest of rewards for this holy activity!

Record any story, instruction, Master Mystic Key or Occultomatic Power Stimulator that you need to absorb more fully. Keep up the habit of marking in your Treasury those sentences and paragraphs which will help you in the future. Apply yourself and your Treasury will yield astounding riches!

> Your next Power is brought to you by the noted psychic researcher Vernon Howard, the founder of miracle-working Psycho-Pictography! Here you will learn how to crystallize your thoughts into material success. With Mr. Howard's help you will learn to channel *all* your new occult and mystic Powers into one single life-fulfilling aim—your SUCCESS!

the psycho-pictography way to a lifetime of success power

*How to Set Up Your Own
Success Program*

Success? Exactly what *is* success? That, obviously, is the first intelligent inquiry we want to make. And the incomparable Mind-Power expert Vernon Howard provides the guiding answer in *Psycho-Pictography: The New Way to Use the Miracle Power of Your Mind*.

You are successful when you really enjoy your life.

There can be no other genuine definition. It digs right to the root of things. A man might make lots of money or get elected to public office or be popular at his club, but what good is all that unless he really enjoys himself? It is of no use whatsoever—and every man and woman inwardly knows it.

The great achievement and the high moral duty of every individual is to be happy through realization of Spiritual Laws.

That is what you will do in this chapter. You will follow the clues to a more successful land for living.

MASTER MYSTIC KEY

Always Put First Things First

People say, "When it comes to success, I never know what I want. One minute it's one thing and the next minute something entirely different. How can I get logical order in my searchings?''

Put first things first.

The first things are always those related to our inner life. Secondary goals are the outward ones, such as our financial activities and our material possessions. By placing the inner life first, we then enjoy the outer! Why not enjoy *yourself* as well as your possessions? This simple thought rarely occurs to millions of intelligent people.

There is nothing wrong with having lots of money; it is just more important to have lots of inner quietness. It is a good idea to redecorate your home; but a far better idea to redecorate the way you think. It is interesting to know the news of the day; it is ten times more interesting to know yourself.

People hesitate to set first things first. It is because they don't realize that inner success is what they *really* want. They fail to see that exterior things are useless substitutes for inner success. A man often achieves a financial fortune and then is surprised to find that he is really no happier than before. Even this shock doesn't wake him up to the fact that his values are all wrong, that he has placed last things first. He usually goes on to a second false assumption: he assumes that some *other* exterior achievement—perhaps fame or power—will do it. But they never will do it. The outer can never do anything for the inner.

It takes genuine daring and courage to set first things first. And it takes a practical mind. People often tell me, ''But Mr. Howard, this is a practical world; we must live in a practical way.''

True. It is for that reason that a man must place his inner riches first! Then—and then only—can he place his exterior affairs in their proper places. And that is when he begins to *enjoy* his success as well as *achieve* it.

This Treasury is designed to help you accomplish exactly this. It puts first things first by providing you with occult and mystic Powers that enhance and bolster your *inner* life. Your outer life will follow your inner pattern!

Now, through Psycho-Pictography, you will learn how to turn your inner into your outer.

QUESTIONS AND ANSWERS ABOUT THE AMAZING POWER OF PSYCHO-PICTOGRAPHY

Question: Exactly what is *Psycho-Pictography?*
Answer: Mr. Howard replies: "*Psycho* indicates the mind, while *Pictography* is the use of pictures to convey an idea. So *Psycho-Pictography* is the use of Mental Pictures to convey spiritual and psychological truths that set a man free."

Question: What is a Mental Picture?
Answer: A Mental Picture is a scene played upon the screen of the mind. The value of Psycho-Pictography, or Mental Pictures, is enormous. You shall see how and why as you go along.

Question: I need about $1300 by the end of this month. Can Psycho-Pictography help me to get it?
Answer: You need money. Someone else needs love. Another needs health. Still another asks for gambling luck. Whatever your need is, Psycho-Pictography will help you—if you learn its principles and apply them.

OCCULTOMATIC POWER STIMULATOR

Learn to use Mental Pictures!
Do you need money? *See* yourself receiving huge sums! Create a Mental Picture of yourself—for example—entering a plush office of a wealthy tycoon. You approach his huge oaken desk, greet him, smile at him. You ask him to invest in your ideas. Watch him draw his checkbook out of the desk drawer, spread it open, lift his pen, and sign a check for you in the amount of, say, $100,000! Take the

check, thank him, and depart, heart pounding with excitement, spirits lifted sky-high.

Do you need a healing? *See* yourself being healed! Create a Mental Picture of yourself—for example—approaching the throne of a Superspiritual Healer. Kneel before him or her. *Feel* his or her hand on you, healing you, making you whole again. And walk away completely healed!

Do you need love? *See* yourself receiving great and lasting love. Create a Mental Picture—for example—of the person you love. See him or her responding to you almost inexorably. He or she cannot help but love you!

Right this minute make yourself a list of needs. Use a blank page in this book for the list or use a separate sheet of paper. *Think first!* What are the immediate needs you need filled? Be specific. Make your list look something like this:

> The landlord willingly and pleasantly excusing me from paying this month's rent on time.
>
> My boss happily giving me a raise.
>
> The man (or woman) I want eagerly falling in love with me.
>
> A contest drawing in which my number is picked for first prize.

Make the list as long as necessary. Don't hesitate to list small as well as big wishes and needs. Then use Mental Pictures in each case. *See* your landlord or boss or sweetheart or healer or contest manager *clearly*. See yourself in their presence and *enact* mentally the entire scene—with the outcome *as you wish it to be!*

Psycho-Pictography will work for you! BELIEVE IT!

AN AMAZING TRUTH ABOUT OCCULT AND MYSTIC POWERS

In reading this book, which plunges deeply into the inner world of man, you may have a question. This question frequently comes up. It is a profitable inquiry with an exciting answer. It goes like this:

"I certainly see the need for exploring my inner world of thoughts and emotions. After all, a man's life is much more than his material possessions. He also lives in his invisible world of desires and sympathies and affections. But I wonder about something. Should we spend too much time in this inner world? Isn't the outer world the practical one?

"To sum up my question, what can all these occult and mystic Powers do for me in the outer world? What is their value? Why should I study them intensely? I'm sincere about this. I really want to know."

If you have felt like asking this question, an amazing truth is about to enter your mind. Welcome it heartily. I guarantee a wealthy reward in everything you do.

Listen!

There is not a single idea in this entire book that doesn't connect directly with your financial affairs. And that connection is favorable to you in a way you cannot presently imagine. But just wait!

If you ever ask, "Are occult and mystic Powers of practical value in my outer world?" I want you to know:

Nothing—absolutely nothing—is more practical.

Relate every Power, including Psycho-Pictography, to your everyday experiences, and you will see how wonderfully practical they are.

With the aid of your Treasury you are setting up your own Success Program. Realize this! Treat each chapter, each Power, as a precious possession. Even as you read and study this present Power of Psycho-Pictography, your subconscious mind is working for you, guiding you to success! Above all, don't flag in your enthusiasm! Your Treasury is like a magnificent castle, each splendid room containing riches and abundance for you.

ALWAYS REMEMBER YOUR CASTLE

People remark, "I get discouraged so easily. Suppose I set up my success program but lose my drive. How can I zoom ahead once more?"

A king was out hunting with his princes in a forest many miles from the castle. A sudden snowstorm fell on the party. In the confusion, the king was separated from the others. When he failed to return to the castle after four days he was given up as lost. But on the fifth day, he appeared in the warm dining room. Someone asked him how he had found strength enough to keep going. The king replied, "I remembered all that the castle means to me."

That kind of thinking will keep anyone going forward. Even while involved in difficulties and obstacles, we can remember what it means to succeed. This remembrance creates a powerful emotional force that carries us through.

It is helpful to concentrate on some specific castle, that is, some special goal of yours. Examples:

> To be less tense and anxious
> To build a brighter future
> To banish depression
> To be a better businessman
> To have smoother human relations.

Think of what it means to win one of these. Remember the rewards that go with your success. This supplies strength that keeps you going all the way to your castle.

You are wiser than you think. You sometimes catch a flash of insight that reveals the truth about things. This flash, coming at an unexpected moment, proves that the truth is already within you and known very well by you. It waits only for your quiet invitation. It is this brief brightness—this Magnificent Glimpse—that is the foundation for all genuine enthusiasm. "A thrill passes through all men at the reception of a new truth . . ." (Emerson).

Pursue this thrill. It is the only enthusiasm that will never wear away, that will never disappoint you. If you will simply permit its intensity to grow, it will do so naturally. Then, you will know an excitement toward life that you have never known before. It is like observing a beautiful sunset: gradually, as the colors rise and spread, they carry you inwardly aloft; you are eager to experience the greater beauty that you know is only a matter of time.

Imprint this truth upon your mind: The study of your Power Chapters is Self-Study, and Self-Study is your key to success in every field of endeavor!

> A man without inner unity is like a group of children at play. They decide to go on a hike, but can't agree on the direction to take. One child calls out for the others to follow him northward, so they all go north for a few yards. Then, a second child calls out that it would be better to go south, so they all switch to the new direction. Back and forth they go, first one way and then another, never getting anywhere. They finally give up in exhaustion and dismay.

A man has thousands of inner parts. He has an emotional center made up of all sorts of desires and inclinations, many of them in opposition to others. His mind contains a vast variety of thoughts and opinions and viewpoints, including negative and contradictory ones. As a man works on himself, say, through self-study, he gathers together all his positive parts into a working unit. These positive forces then harmonize consistently and for persistent purpose. The man becomes like an automobile engine whose parts are assembled into a power-plant capable of carrying the car wherever desired. Such a man has genuine will.

How to achieve this inner unity that supplies will-power? First, realize that it is quite possible for you to pull yourself together! Then, carefully study all the Powers in this Treasury. Your unity is their purpose.

HOW TO ENJOY YOUR VOYAGE

You must not worry over your progress. Whether you sail toward a material goal or a psychological one, anxiety has absolutely no place in your plans. How can you break the connection between your mind and worry?

By enjoying the trip itself. By abandoning all ideas that you are responsible for keeping things going.

> A young man found himself stranded in Japan. Thinking he might work his way back home on a merchant ship, he applied to the captain. His offer was accepted. On the sailing date he reported to the captain and asked, "What should I do?"
>
> "Just enjoy the voyage," the captain answered.
>
> "Enjoy the voyage?" repeated the puzzled young man.
>
> "Yes. That's all you need to do. Your passage has already been paid."
>
> It developed that a friend had heard of the problem and had paid the fare home.

Likewise, there is nothing we need to do or really can do except to enjoy the trip. As long as we are aboard the ship, that is, if we are traveling along with the right principles, we can completely relax. The ship is headed in the right direction, and so are we. Oh, yes, the voyage might include some stormy emotions for a while, or we may be rocked by mental confusions, but that is not really a problem. The Truth is always intact, and so are we.

We must rid our minds of the idea that we are responsible for results. That is a tremendous contribution to your sense of relaxation.

Make up your mind to enjoy the voyage. Sooner or later, your mind will agree that it's a great idea.

It is your moral duty to be happy.

MAKING THE PERFECT START

Wherever you want to achieve a new success, you can make a perfect start. Whether in your business affairs or domestic life or mental world, you can make a start that ends successfully. The start of a new project needs close examination because it sometimes creates a mental crisis. People ask, "Where should I start?" and "How can I persist?" and "What should I do?"

I want to show you how to answer all these questions. Just follow as many of these rules as you can.

Whenever you start a new project:

1. Know exactly what you want.
2. Be confident of your inner forces.
3. Collect all available information.
4. Dismiss wasteful and negative attitudes.
5. Score a series of small successes.
6. Harmonize with natural laws of success.
7. Cease pointless actions.
8. Make the most of every opportunity.
9. Concentrate on one area at a time.
10. Enjoy your new project.

Suppose that you want to start a new program in your relations with other people. You want to understand people better. You wish to attract new friends, customers, associates. You desire to be more attractive to others. Well, you can get off to a good start with any or all of the above points.

Take point 3; why not begin a regular reading program with your 13 Power chapters? For point 6, you can review the dynamic laws of success which dot these pages. Take point 9; why not concentrate on your *favorite* Power for a period of seven days?

What can you do right now?

You can start!

HOW JAMES L. USES PSYCHO-PICTOGRAPHY TO ENRICH HIS LIFE

Here is James L.'s report, word for word:

"I *enjoy* using Mental Pictures, so I use them for everything. And I mean *everything*! From the minute I get up in the morning till I go to bed at night, I use Mental Pictures. Why not? My mind would be idle otherwise. Or gathering wool!

"I don't know from one minute to the next how my exercises will work. I admit it. But, it's marvelous the way they work! I mentally picture myself getting promoted on my job. I use Mental Pictures to meet girls. I pictured a brand new car for about a month. When my parents were talking about divorce, I used Psycho-Pictography to get them back together again.

"Does it work? I'll say it works! Oh, I didn't get the *exact* model of car I wanted, but, let me tell you, my new wheels are spiffy, sporty and attractive to girls! My parents are acting like honeymooners! I've got the job I've always wanted! And money? My bank account is fat! Best of all—I'm happy! That's all I have to say."

WATCH YOUR OWN PROGRESS

Perhaps you say, "I am studying the principles of Psycho-Pictography with you. Will I actually see myself thinking and acting in a new and better way? If so, how does it all come about?"

This hits upon one of the vital purposes of Psycho-Pictography: *Change. Self-change.* It always happens whenever you sincerely apply yourself. Self-change, a fresh way of thinking, is a great aim of Mental Pictures. It is an aim we must not miss.

It is strange how a person can study a truthful system for many years, perhaps attend countless classes, and yet remain the same kind of person inwardly. Such a person has missed the entire point—that of inner transformation. Such a man may be uneasy over the fact that he still has the same old worries and pains, but he never stops to ask himself *why* he remains in the same old rut. He must wake up and challenge himself.

It is not enough to hear the truth. We must openly receive it. The great clue is *receptivity*. Then, the received truth sets us free. It changes us. We become new. And so do our circumstances.

You can actually see yourself change for the better. It is observable magic. This change is seen by comparison. You discern that you are less anxious today than you were yesterday. You see definite improvement in the way you meet a crisis. You behave in a different and superior manner.

> Suppose you decide to walk up the stairs of a ten-story building. You pause at the fifth floor to look out the window. At this fifth-story level, you can see a certain amount of the city. When you climb to the tenth floor, you see much more. You know that you are in a superior position because you can compare the two levels. Because you have changed your position, you increase the amount of the city to be enjoyed. This is observable success.

As you work with Psycho-Pictography, you will see actual changes. Incidents that formerly upset you will lose their negative power. Vague apprehensions will give way to tranquility. You will see, perhaps for the first time, that everything is really all right.

> All our progress is an unfolding, like the vegetable bud. You have first an instinct, then an opinion, then a knowledge, as the plant has root, bud, and fruit. Trust the instinct to the end, though you can render no reason. It is vain to hurry it. By trusting it to the end, it shall ripen into truth and you shall know why you believe. (Emerson)

POWER-POINTERS

1. What is success? First and last, it is personal happiness.

2. Place first things first. Success follows.

3. Nothing is of more practical value to you in your everyday life than mystic and occult Powers.

4. Connect the ideas of Psycho-Pictography to every area of your life. They are best friends.

5. You are wiser than you think. As we rid our minds of false notions, wisdom springs up like an underground stream.

6. Self-unity is self-Power.

7. Review the ideas in this Power-chapter. Let them enrich you.

8. Do not burden yourself with worry over results. Enjoy your voyage toward your goals. Enjoy your Powers.

9. Remember that mystic and occult Powers are resident within you at all times; all you have to do is activate them. Visualize yourself receiving great Powers from a revered Holy Man. This is Psycho-Pictography at work.

10. Expect change in yourself and in your environment, as well as in your financial condition, your love life, your luck, your personality, YOUR ENTIRE EXISTENCE!

Editor's Note on Power #13

Make a comprehensive list of your needs, desires, wishes, dreams and goals. Then right beside it list a set of Mental Pictures which will help you achieve your ends. Like this:

Desire	*Mental Picture*
Marriage	You are sitting with her (him) in candlelight, soft music playing in the background. He (she) is yielding to your every wish.

Luck	You are in Las Vegas. Play the roulette wheel, poker, Blackjack. Whatever you do, see yourself winning at an alarming rate! Always!
Friendship	Picture yourself meeting new, exciting, and responsive people who want to help you, enjoy your company, and want to be near you.
Health	Envision yourself naked, vibrating with health, standing beneath an all-embracing Sun, its powerful rays emanating strength, vitality and health.
Riches	Enjoy the Mental Picture of yourself discovering buried treasure, gems, gold, uranium, oil! Be imaginative! Be bold! Try picturing yourself walking through a field of clover in the rain—but it's raining $100 bills!

Add to this list yourself—*in writing!* For each wish you make, list a strong and emotive Mental Picture to fulfill it. Use your new Power of Psycho-Pictography as a tool!

You now possess all the Powers you will need to enrich, enliven, and enhance your entire life. Your Parker Lifetime Treasury of Mystic and Occult Powers is now complete, at your beck and call, ready to provide you with the Power you need to accomplish almost anything.

Go on now to check your Prosperity Progress.

YOUR PARKER PROSPERITY PROGRESS REPORT #3

As with the other Progress Reports, this final Report is designed to:

1. Test your absorption of the ideas and methods set forth in your Parker Treasury of Mystic and Occult Powers.

2. Refresh your memory of certain key ideas and Power-evincing concepts.

This final Report scans through the entire Treasury, but most of the questions which follow are keyed to the last four Power-chapters.

Instructions:

There follow 10 multiple-choice questions. Write down your choice of *a*, *b*, *c* or *d*, in your Personal Power Notebook. Each correct answer is worth 10 points. A final score of less than 50 is Poor. A score of 50-60 is Fair; 60-70 is Good; 70-80 is Very Good; 80-90 is Excellent; and a score over 90 is Superior. Now choose the correct answer to each of the following:

I. To unleash your latent mental Powers you should
   a. Take vitamins
   b. Become a Yogi
   c. Stop feeling inferior to others
   d. Go into a trance

II. To most of us breathing is simply inhaling and exhaling. To the Ancient Masters, however, it is infinitely more. In fact, they do not speak of "breathing" at all; they speak of
   a. Karma
   b. Nirvana
   c. Kundalini
   d. Prana

III. Many people who today enjoy luxury, comfort, and riches
   a. Worked and slaved to earn their position
   b. Simply attracted money like a magnet
   c. Got ahead by unfair and illegal means
   d. Inherited their status

IV. Occult and Mystic Magic is
   a. Disproven by science

b. The pipedream of idle minds

c. Beyond logic as science knows it

d. The domain of qualified magicians

V   When you consecrate your Meditation Stone and transform it into a Power Amulet, you have

a. A very nice piece of jewelry

b. Something to pass around for friends to look at

c. A lovely conversation piece

d. A vehicle of mystic and occult Power

VI. Many people today harbor an old superstitious fear of mysticism and occultism but, actually, as your Treasury proves, occultism

a. Deals with the positive spectrum of cosmic Power

b. Makes you a success at parties

c. Is more fearful than people imagine

d. Has no value at all

VII. You were created to know and experience true love. For every person there is a true soul mate. When you once learn how to use the laws of Mind Cosmology, you can

a. Turn people into sex slaves

b. Magnetize and attract your true soul mate in love and marriage

c. Easily steal another person's husband or wife

d. Become a Black Magician

VIII. Aside from the material benefits enjoyed by many astral travelers, there is this common report:

a. You can be a voyeur without fearing detection

b. You can rob a bank and never be seen

c. You *know* you will live after your body has been buried in the ground

d You can become a famous nightclub entertainer

IX   There is only one genuine definition of success that digs right to the root of things. It is

a. You are successful when you really enjoy your life
b. You are successful when others bow to your wishes
c You are successful when you possess fame and fortune
d You are successful when people beg for your help

X. To get the most out of your Parker Lifetime Treasury of Mystic and Occult Powers, you should
    a. Read it through and then give it to someone else in need
    b. Study and practice each Power carefully and diligently
    c. Skip the chapters that have no appeal
    d. None of the above

Here's How to Rate Your Answers:

The correct answers are: I-c; II-d; III-b; IV-c; V-d; VI-a; VII-b; VIII-c; IX-a; X-b.

Now score yourself, taking 10 points for each right answer. Allow no score for questions answered incorrectly or for questions not answered.

Record your Progress directly in your Personal Power Notebook.

My Prosperity Progress Report Score is ———————.

A FINAL WORD: HOW TO MAKE YOUR MYSTIC AND OCCULT POWERS LAST YOUR LIFETIME

You are not holding in your hands a mere book. This is a *Treasury*. And, like a king's treasury, it should be consulted each and every time you need aid. When a king needs money or jewels, he goes to his treasure-house and withdraws the amount needed to further enhance his life and kingdom. You will do the same with this Treasury of mystic and occult Powers.

You may confidently expect your Prosperity Progress to increase. As your Powers increase, so does your prosperity increase.

You may have noticed that each Power in your Treasury is personalized—each becomes YOUR Power. These 13 Powers will stand you in good stead as potent allies if you will treat them as treasured personal possessions. The best way to do this, I think, is to set up a program of study for yourself. For example, for instant and spontaneous results, start a 13-day streamlined Program of Progress by studying one Power each day. To reinforce this immediate regime, set up a 13-week Study Program of Power. And to reinforce even that, set up a 13-month Power Program, taking one chapter a month into your psyche.

Your Study and Practice Program should look something like this:

1st day, week or month: Unleash your secret mental Power by studying Chapter One. Learn the importance of rest. Eliminate those mental distortions that limit your Power. *Practice* the Master Mystic Key to constructive "daydreaming." Study the Three Steps of the Miracle Mind Magic Stimulator and *put them to work in your daily life*. Increase your Mental Power by following the instructions in the Occultomatic Power Stimulator. *Take notes*.

2nd day, week or month: Learn how to awaken the Fiery Serpent of Psychic Energy in yourself. Cultivate your "sixth sense" by following the instructions in Power #2, reviewing all Questions and Answers. Absorb the meaning and importance of Prana-breathing. Make a list of your goals and go after them with new Mental Power. Learn the ten basic desires that motivate all human action—and make these desires brighten your life! The instructions on how to make your Astral Body your friend and guide will help you to accomplish all things. Study each section of this mighty Power carefully and write down ideas as they occur to you.

3rd day, week or month: Money can be yours. Never doubt it! Study Power #3 and learn how to pyramid wealth with mystic money Power as outlined for you by the remarkable occultist Norvell. Remember the importance of meeting and influencing prominent and wealthy people. This mystic Power will embolden you, empower you, and delight you with amazing results—if you will absorb its message and practice it daily. Study the facts and fallacies about money magnetism. You *can* be a money magnet with this

Power. Act upon the Occultomatic Power Stimulator in this Power-chapter.

4th day, week or month: Learn the colorful secrets that will bring you the miracle of metaphysical healing. Even if you are healthy, *study this chapter*. You will learn how to heal others—friends, loved ones, acquaintances, even strangers. Remember: **to** heal others unselfishly is to insure your own good health *for a lifetime*! Get familiar with the correspondence between color and certain illnesses. You will find this knowledge precious throughout your life.

5th day, week or month: Practice the Magic of Power #5. Study, write down, absorb, and imprint on your subconscious mind the 10 fast-working runic spells that will magically smooth your path through life. These potent spells provided by Malak will serve you well in coming years. They are safe here in your Treasury and will be like new each time you pick it up—today, tomorrow, next week, next year, *ten years from now*! This is your private and secret wealth of amazing and miracle-working Powers. Treasure it!

6th day, week or month: Apply yourself to the mystic knowledge in your sixth Power and learn how to *command* Lady Luck for hidden treasure and fabulous fortune. Study the Questions and Answers, pay attention to the Master Mystic Key, learn the Morris plan for your control and command of phenomenal good luck. That's what this Luck Power is for—YOU!

7th day, week or month: Concentrate at this time on the titanic new Avatar Power rituals provided for you by the great mystic Geof Gray-Cobb. Make Avatar Power yours; use it often, daily, weekly, monthly—get acquainted with it as you are acquainted with your own name. Make it a frequent companion on your journey through this life and it will help you to change misery into happiness, lack into plenty, sorrow into joy. Use your mirror to become familiar with the invisible Power Gates within you—and let this Power-chapter activate those Gates for you.

8th day, week or month: Utilize the remarkable Power of Hypno-Cybernetics that virtually guarantees achieving your goals.

Why should you fall short of your full potential when you have such Powers as this one at your disposal? Study the Master Mystic Key, learn to use the magic Power of pretending. With the controlled imagination, as this Power teaches you, you can achieve anything in this life—*all* your life! Just practice the six easy steps to the Power of H-C and it will work for you as it has worked for thousands of others. Learn to de-program negativity and to program positivity into your entire psychic system with the help of powerful H-C.

9th day, week or month: Put White Witchcraft knowledge to work for you! Study Power #9 whenever you can. Learn how to make and use amulets, talismans and charms for protection, mystic Powers and good luck. Enjoy your life by absorbing this occult knowledge completely and carrying it with you every step of the way through this life. If you should forget something, do not hesitate to review the Power-chapter. Get your stone, consecrate it, and USE IT! Construct your Power Medallion according to the easy instructions. You will be amazed what wonders this mystic aid can work in your life.

10th day, week or month: By all means concentrate on Norvell's regime for releasing your occult Power in Chapter 10. This is your reinforcement Power, remember. Study the Questions and Answers to familiarize yourself with this potent Power, learn the polarities of occult Power, and then, implementing the Occulto-matic Power Stimulator, dedicate yourself as a positive channel for creative occult Power. Once you become adept in this Power it will fortify you throughout your remaining years.

11th day, week or month: Love will be yours if you will apply yourself to the teachings in Chapter 11—how to magnetize, attract, and command love. From this moment until the day you depart this old earth you will not suffer loneliness or solitude, but will be ever in the company of a loved one. Employ the five points in the Master Mystic Key and learn how to construct the proper astral image of your heart's desire. This Power will not bring only you love but you will be able to command love to enter any life you choose. Think of the multitude of people you can help with this Power! The more love you send out, the more love you receive!

12th day, week or month: The Power to astral travel at will is a fantastic Power to possess. Study Chapter 12 slowly, with pen or pencil in hand to make notes in your Personal Power Notebook, and absorb this remarkable knowledge of other worldly Power. Follow to the letter the instruction in the Master Mystic Key as set forth by the occult expert Al G. Manning. His lifelong labor is condensed into this one potent Chapter for you. Read the Questions and Answers, absorb the essence of this Power, and prepare yourself for Astral Travel. There isn't a day in your life from this moment on, that you won't be able to avail yourself of this wonder-working Power.

13th day, week or month: Your Treasury is designed to bring you a *lifetime* of success. And so is this occult thirteenth chapter: Psycho-Pictography. Learn Howard's method of using Mental Pictures for a lifetime of success Power. Study this Power-chapter carefully, diligently, and with enthusiasm and anticipation, because when you learn this mental method of transforming life, you will be delighted to see everything you touch turn to gold.

> Somewhere in the heart of every individual, there is a fervent desire for the things of which your Treasury speaks. Yet few people ever come to enjoy the fruits of their desires. This shall no longer be true for you. You have in your hands at this moment the key to a life more abundant—for now and for always! All people need today is Power—occult and mystic Power—and now you have it—here and now! In time, if you apply yourself, you will discover that you possess not only thirteen separate, mighty Powers, but ONE, UNENDING, INDEFATIGABLE, LIFE/LASTING P* O * W * E * R. Enjoy it!